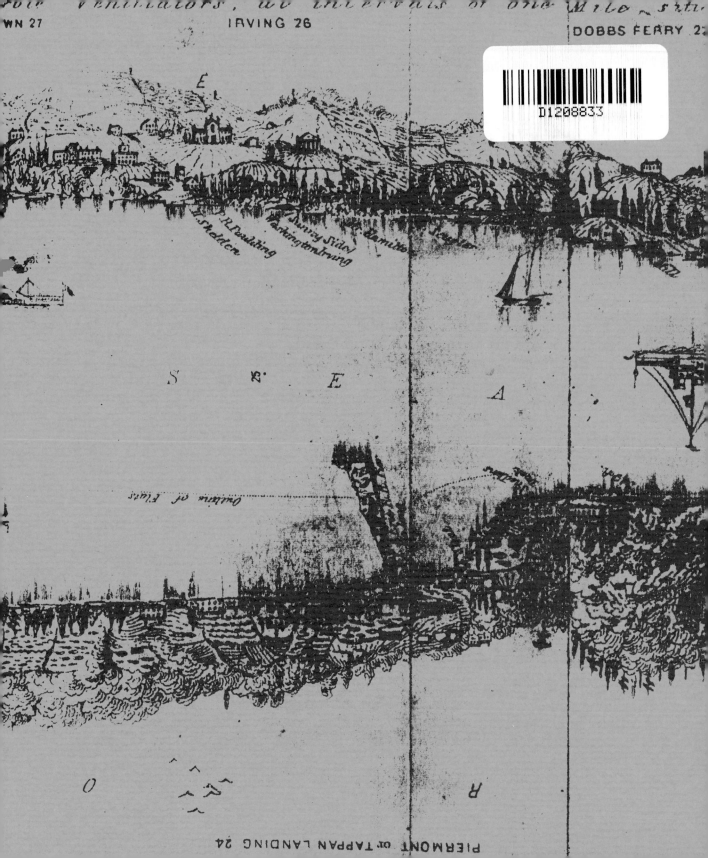

Wolfert's Roost when Irving purchased it

PORTRAIT OF A VILLAGE

Wolfert's Roost

IRVINGTON-ON-HUDSON

THE WASHINGTON IRVING PRESS
Irvington-on-Hudson, N.Y.

Copyright © 1971, 1979 by The Washington Irving Press, Inc.; © 1997 by Trustees of the Irvington Public Library. Third Edition. All rights reserved.

Grateful acknowledgement is made to the following for permission to reprint the works listed:

Thomas Y. Crowell Company for pages 92–94 from *Helen Gould Was My Mother-in-Law* by Celeste Andrews Seton. Copyright 1953 by Celeste Andrews Seton and Clark Andrews

University of North Carolina Press for excerpts from *Gentleman's Progress: The Itinerarium of Dr. Alexander Hamilton—1744,* edited with an introduction by Carl C. Bridenbaugh. Copyright 1948 by the University of North Carolina Press

Random House, Inc., Alfred A. Knopf, Inc. for "The Ghost of the River Octagon" from *The Screaming Ghost and Other Stories* by Carl Carmer. Copyright © 1956 by Carl Carmer, and for "Father Wakes Up the Village" reprinted from *The Best of Clarence Day.* Copyright 1935 and renewed 1962 by Katherine B. Day

John Black Brady for *I Remember* by Jennie Prince Black. Copyright 1938

Special illustrations for the volume include:

Binding: The foot of Main Street as it appeared about 1880

End papers: A section of the river, from "Panorama of the Hudson River—New York to Albany", by William Wade, 1846

Title pages: A four foot model of a portion of Main Street, Irvington, as it appeared in 1950, by Laurence Lustig

Line drawings: On pages 13, 16, 20, 23, 26, 33, 58, 129, 135 by Lauri Denyer Marder

Library of Congress catalog number 77-180730

ISBN 0-9603508

Printed in the United States of America by Quinn-Woodbine, Inc.

Foreword

THE VILLAGE OF IRVINGTON on the shores of the Hudson River in New York has been fortunate in the men and women who over the years have enjoyed her, served her, and above all for our purposes, written about her.

In essence this book seeks through their writings to sketch a portrait of a village, not to write its history. Insofar as possible people speak from the past—directly by their writings or by telling of events as they have lived them, foreshadowing the village of today.

Chronology has had its place; we have used dates where they were necessary, but more often the clock of the years will be internal. We have tried to keep necessary explanatory matter and other connective tissue to a minimum. Mainly the book is a patchwork, an album of what people have done on the nearly 2000 acres that make up the village of Irvington.

A word about the origins of the project. For a number of years before his death in 1952 Arthur C. Lord, long identified with Irvington, took a lively interest in the village and its background and developed a substantial amount of solid historical information about Irvington and its past.

Following Arthur Lord's work Wolfert Ecker Lockwood, a descendant of one of Irvington's earliest families, went on to build his own truly encyclopedic knowledge of the village. His work was still in progress when he died in 1969. His notes and papers, his sources, references, and his collection of photographs, generously made available by his family, were his legacy to the village he

Wolfert Lockwood enjoying his working costume as Host-Farmer at the Philipsburg Manor restoration. Irvington's historian, he had also been a Village Trustee, and President of the Board of Education

loved. Much of his work is recorded in this volume, either directly or as a source. Mr. Lockwood's family has given permission to elide or combine his material at points. To make the mechanics of quotation less obtrusive, we have prefaced, but not identified further, the many quotations from Mr. Lockwood with his initials "WEL."

The project owes more to Mr. Lockwood, however, than that substantial debt. His tireless documentation and his affection for Irvington were truly the origins of this book.

Jennie Prince Black, who came to the village as a child just as the 1870's were beginning, has left a lively, sunny memoir of Irvington, as she put it, "of the Dignified Seventies, the Elegant Eighties, and the Gay Nineties." We have quoted often from her book, *I Remember.*

Another colorful memoir of Irvington from which we have quoted is Isabel K. Benjamin's *From Dawn to Twilight.*

Finally, since this project is in a real sense a communal endeavor—put together not only from documented records but from letters, scrapbooks, photographs, and reminiscences for all of which the editors are deeply grateful—it is impossible to give acknowledgments fully or even adequately.

We would be remiss, however, if we did not express our thanks especially to Mrs. Wolfert Lockwood for making available Mr. Lockwood's papers; to Mr. John Black Brady for permission to make full use of his grandmother's book; and to Miss Caroline Dutcher for making available *The Old Home by the River,* the memoir by her great-grandfather, the Reverend Jacob Dutcher; and to Musya S. Sheeler (Mrs. Charles Sheeler) for her photographs that make up the "Family Album."

Those who have worked most actively in compiling and producing this book are:

EDITORIAL ADVISOR
Carl Carmer

EDITORS
Text—Polly Anne Graff, Stewart Graff
Graphics—Barbara Denyer, Carolyn Ramirez

BOOK DESIGN
Laurence Lustig

PUBLISHER
John P. R. Budlong

Irvington, New York, October 1971

Left, Jennie Prince Black
Center, Arthur C. Lord
Right, Musya S. Sheeler

Table
of Contents

October on the Tappan Zee. Painting by J. H. Archer, 1869

Introduction
to a village

CARL CARMER SPEAKS of Irvington:

My home town, Irvington-on-Hudson, was named many years ago in honor of a distinguished writer and a beautiful river. I have felt that something of the sunny geniality of Washington Irving, one of the nation's earliest and most delightful tellers of tales, was forever imparted to the neighborhood in which he lived. His home still stands here and has been restored to the spic-and-span condition in which his charming nieces kept it for their bachelor uncle in the early nineteenth century days when he was alive. Like many another old American house, it is an amusing mixture of architectural influences—Dutch, English, Chinese, Moorish, and yet it seems to have an artistic unity of its own. It is easy to believe that the whimsically creative mind that fashioned the story of Rip Van Winkle or the ballad-like tale of the Headless Horseman found joy in this curious dwelling, "Sunnyside," on the banks of the Hudson.

As for the wide river, it is an ever-present backdrop for the doings of the community. Since most of these begin on Main Street, and since Main Street slants straight down, between an aisle of spreading shade trees, to the glinting water's edge, the stream seems almost inseparable from the town—a constantly exerted influence.

Main Street is our principal business street, but it is not wholly devoted to trade, for perhaps a score of private residences still linger on it. Aside from its view of the river, it might pass for any other American Main Street in a town of comparable size. Just above its upper end lies a sloping meadow where cows are pastured during the summer months. The street drops down toward the river from Broadway, a north-south street running near the river all the way from New York City to the state capital city, Albany. At either side of the down-sloping pavement stand neat business buildings erected for the most part not less than two generations ago.

As for the rest of Main Street, it holds a schoolhouse; a town hall containing, besides the rooms devoted to local government, a library and the police department; a firehouse; a community center; a number of well-supplied food stores (for the most part of the "chain" variety); a drug store; two banks; many small specialized shops; and, at the foot by the river, a railroad station. The town's major industry has been for many years down by the river, where it makes boilers, heaters, and glass greenhouses—the kind that professional florists use.

Irvington is only twenty miles from Manhattan Island and the skyscrapers of New York. It has over six thousand inhabitants, many of whom are determined that it shall have few more. It is a green and shady village, and a village they are determined it shall remain! In the mid-nineteenth century days when there were no automobiles, the land on which Irvington stands was oc-

Pasture on Broadway

cupied by the big country estates of men who had grown rich in the city of New York. Now these vast tracts are no more. In their places stand residential areas usually designated as parks—Ardsley, Matthiessen, Jaffray, Spiro, and Barney—each a cluster of pleasant houses set among green lawns. Along the bank of the river stretches a modern cooperative apartment development called "Half Moon," and the inhabitants enjoy uninterrupted views of the majestic Hudson from their terraces and balconies. There are several other attractive apartment communities in other sections of the village.

The village has a quiet, democratic life of its own. As in most small communities, the Board of Trustees has difficult problems to solve which, despite its part-time nature, it

Town Hall. The deed prohibited "spirituous liquors" on the premises. The builders made their own secret protest. They sealed a pint of whiskey in the tower where it remains.

handles efficiently and with good humor and dispatch. The spirit of its salaried employees is much the same on a full-time basis. The volunteer Fire Department has such a fine reputation that the town considers admission to it a signal honor. Hence, there is usually a waiting list of applicants for membership. When the fire sirens sound, the village is suddenly alive with running men dashing for their places on the Department's motor vehicles.

A walk on Main Street from the Hudson River to Broadway

A 1970 GRADUATE of Irvington High School feels the pervasiveness of the river and looks at his village:

Irvington is poised above a body of water. The Hudson River is thirty miles inland from the ocean. It freezes during the winter. On most days, it is grey and slow—and during this winter, the ice is swept down the river in floes, or it eddies into the coves—and now and again comes the sound of ice breaking or shifting. From all over Irvington, from the oddest vantages, one will see the river: on a road while turning a bend, on the top of a water tower, in the salon of a ruined mansion, in a livingroom and through the plate glass windows. Once, it was seven seasons ago, I wrote in another piece about the Hudson: "If you were caught in a pinch without clothes you could swim in the Hudson and cover your nakedness with grease." Swimming in the Hudson one will notice that the water tastes like light machine oil, but that it is warm and that there is algae in the water, and the river bottom is soft and covered over with silt.

Especially from Main Street, the river is ever and unavoidably in one's eyes. Main Street leads on a straight line down to the river. The river is important to Main Street, and Main Street is important to the town. To know the town one must know Main Street, to understand Main Street one must understand the river. Therefore, as we walk up Main Street, keep the river in mind, remain aware that it is behind you and even at one's back.

We shall see very little on this winter's day, for Irvington is not a museum piece; there is little worthwhile to see. Unlike visiting a battlefield, one may not derive satisfaction from a knowledge of the ferocity of gone-by events. Unlike touring a graveyard, one may not grow sensible to the silences, for the exhausts of passing cars and the tolling of the town bells shall interfere with silent communions. Unlike witnessing a pyramid, no ragged and vain presence will impress one to tears when the numbers of grandeur and slaves are recited. We shall only be looking at a small town. A small town on a half-mile stretch of road.

". . . the river is ever and unavoidably in one's eyes"

"Here was Broadway..."

AN EARLIER DESCRIPTION of the village is Jennie Prince Black's account of her family's arrival in Irvington in the 1870's:

It took us fully four hours to go as far as Irvington from New York City even with a good pair of horses. But we stopped at a hotel in Yonkers called the Getty House for luncheon and reached our new home on Broadway about three o'clock in the afternoon. With poor roads and mud almost up to the hubs of our carriage—as it was in early spring—it was a laborious, but also a beautiful, journey.

Here was Broadway, with its tall, interlacing trees on either side—it seemed as though we drove through noble archways.

The magnificent residences on either side of the only highway, so many of the lawns on the western side sloping down to the river bank. On the east side of the driveway quite a few of the high mansions commanded a view of the Hudson from The Highlands to the high buildings in New York City.

Several lanes ran down between these large estates to the river. Main Street was the center of our neat, clean, charming little village which boasted many old houses and a few shops. A building used for our Town Councils stood on the site of the present Town Hall. The Public School was a small brick house south of Main Street on Broadway; three churches and two Presbyterian mission chapels, one at Dublin (a little Irish settlement now East Irvington), the other at Penny Bridge.

Penny Bridge was the old boundary line between Irvington and Tarrytown. It was a small bridge across a brook (in reality a row of planks) which must have been a thorn in the flesh in Revolutionary times to each

A postcard of Dublin, settled by the Irish workers who built the old Croton Aqueduct. The section became East Irvington

Free Public Library backed by the "Mental and Moral Improvement Society," later housed next door in the Atheneum. No Irvington resident had the two year certificate required for librarian

passer-by, for he was delayed and obliged to pay one penny before he might proceed on his way.

The bridge has long since vanished but the brook still runs down the hill and under the Broadway traffic and bounds merrily on to the river.

————

Irvington, like any village, had an earlier history than written accounts record . . .

The once and sometime Mauritius

THE BEGINNING WAS THE RIVER.

From Lake Tear of the Clouds, high in the Adirondacks, the Hudson River sets its three-hundred-mile course. Gathering force in the broad uplands, flowing almost due south, it cuts the great range of Appalachian Mountains and flows imperiously on to the sea. In turn the sea sends back its salt waters with the ebb and flow of the tides.

It was a river of changing names through the early years when only the Indians roamed and camped along its shores. The Delawares called it the *Mohicanittuk*, the Mohicans the *Shatamuc*, and the Iroquois the *Cohohatatea*. When the Dutch came they called the river *Mauritius* after Prince Maurice of Orange. Later it was spoken of as the *North River*. And finally, of course, it became the *Hudson*.

Indians knew the river as a source of food and as a strategic waterway. Beginning with its exploration in 1609 by Henry Hudson, the Dutch and then the English—explorers, fur-traders, settlers—used it as a highway.

Long before the disappearance of the Indians the Hudson had new settlers, as a contemporary observed: "lured by the sweet land, the river full of fishes and a great store of salmen, and countless oyster beds, and by the inland stands of timber—pine, hickory, chestnut, oak and maple." About 1680, on the eastern shore of the Hudson, some twenty-five miles and a bit more from the busy Dutch-English town of New York on the Southern tip of Manhattan Island, the first settlement took root in the location that is now Irvington.

"A View in Hudson's River of the entrance of what is called the Topan Sea" sketched by his Excellency Gov. Pownal, published in London, 1761

Lords
and ladies

Portrait by John Wollaston, presumably of the third Frederick Philipse, last Lord of the Manor, who was "attainted of treason in 1779, ordered banished from the state and his property confiscated."

THE FIRST HUDSON RIVER farms were almost entirely bits of the manor lands granted so openhandedly by the British Crown to a few privileged residents of the colony. The settlers of the acres that were later to be the village of Irvington were tenants, farming pieces of the vast manorial holdings of Frederick Philipse, and paying rents to the lord of the manor, for the most part in kind.

Frederick Philipse's rise to position in the colony had been spectacular. His family had come originally from Bohemia. His grandfather, a viscount, Protestant in sympathy, had been forced to flee during the religious wars, and the family had settled in the little town of Bolsward on Holland's northwestern shore. There Frederick Philipse was born in 1626, an only son.

Frederick learned the trade of carpenter, but he must have been restless at the lack of opportunity to practice it. In the mid 1650's, when he was in his late twenties, he emigrated with his parents to New York. There the way was open for his energy and abilities. Using the skill of his trade as a base, he became the official carpenter of the Dutch West India Company. Seemingly he functioned also as a builder and as an architect. He branched out into trade to become one of the city's leading merchants. City surveyor, alderman, warden in the Dutch Church, the path led on to membership on the Governor's Council by 1682.

Two marriages in no way hindered. The first was to the redoubtable Margaret De Vries, a widow whose own tough-mindedness contributed in large share to the substantial dowry she brought him. Her first husband had been a successful fur trader, and she had accompanied him on the lonely voyages along the coast to trade for fur covered hides as well as on the trips to Europe to sell the rare, soft furs. Her servants on land and the crews on her ships came to acknowledge her iron hand. Before her death in 1691 she bore three children by Philipse, and the inheritance of the manor lands was assured.

Philipse married again in 1692 to another wealthy widow, Catherine Derval, a sister of Stephanus Van Cortlandt, the first lord of the Cortlandt Manor.

The manor that Frederick Philipse was to have confirmed to him in 1693 by charter from King William and Queen Mary of England extended from North Tarrytown to the Bronx, and from the Hudson River on the west to the Bronx River on the east. In part this royal charter served to give Philipse title

Dutch Patroon

beyond question to lands he had already bought from the Indians.

In 1681 he had purchased a first portion of what was to become the manor holdings. Four months later, in 1682, he bought a tract of land running southward along the Hudson. Within this section would be Irvington.

The occasion of the purchase was solemn, with the formalities carefully observed. Leading Indian sachems were present. The purchase price is detailed:

Twelve fathoms of black wampum
Twelve fathoms of duffels (a coarse cloth)
Twelve blankets
Ten guns
Fifty pounds of powder
Eight coats
Thirty bars of lead
Twelve shirts
Twelve pairs of stockings
Thirty hoes
Two ankers of rum
Twenty boxes
Two and a half vats of beer
Three drawing knives
Two coopers adz
Ten earthen jugs
Ten axes
Eight fathoms of stoud Water cloth, for blankets
Fifty knives
Twelve kettles

Philipse immediately began the organization of his holdings. He built the manor hall that still stands in Yonkers, together with a grist mill, on the banks of the Nepperhan River. At the northern end of his estate, on the shores of the Pocantico River, in North Tarrytown, he also erected a manor house and mill, a complex recently restored.

And farmers

IT WAS ESSENTIAL that the river lands be cleared for farming, and within a few years, before the turn of the century (1700), names still familiar in Irvington began to appear on the rent rolls of the manor as tenant farmers. For the next hundred years, until the end of the Revolutionary War and beyond, these farms made up the physical pattern of what is now Irvington.

The first tenants were of Dutch extraction. Wolfert Lockwood in the draft of his history of Irvington wrote:

[WEL]

Wolfert Ecker, whose parents had come from Holland, is listed as a resident of the Philipse land in 1692; his occupation is given as that of a tub maker [cooper] and he was listed as well on the tax rolls of the manor as a farmer.

———

The beautifully situated Ecker farmhouse was to become the nucleus for Washington Irving's home.

[WEL]

Immediately to the south was a farm comprising most of the present-day Irvington's Matthiessen Park and Main Street areas, held by Barent Dutcher, born in Kingston about 1675 of parents who had also emigrated from Holland. Dutcher erected his home on a rise of land overlooking the Tappan Zee.

About the turn of the century the name of Captain John Buckhout appeared on the rent rolls of the manor. He is believed to have been a captain in the colonial militia and to have served in one of the many wars with France along with his neighbor to the south, Captain Jan Harmse.

Captain Buckhout married twice, lived to the age of 103, and left the prodigious number of 240 descendants when he died in 1785. He was the only one of the original tenant farmers to live through the long span of time that ended with the Revolution.

Captain Harmse cleared the land south of his neighbor Buckhout and erected his house which still stands on a corner of

Captain John's grave in Sleepy Hollow Cemetery, North Tarrytown

One of the first tenant farmhouses, the Buckhout house on the river shore just south of what became the village center

Broadway in the village. His farm extended from the Hudson to the Sawmill River.

The way of living on the land that is now Irvington must have seemed as changeless as the cycles of planting, nurturing, harvesting and preserving that repeated themselves year after year. But the land was a part of the Hudson Valley, and the Hudson Valley was a highway to the north. For almost a hundred years after Frederick Philipse received his lordly grant, the thrust would be northward. Change did not come rapidly to the farms along the river's banks, but, however slowly, the valley became a great transportation artery. Along its length flowed forces that would secure the frontiers to the north, help to channel a nation westward and to create at river's end one of the world's great port cities, New York.

The road

FOR MORE THAN A CENTURY after Henry Hudson's *Half Moon* nosed uncertainly upstream the river was the only highway northward from Manhattan. But the Hudson's tides were strong and its winds capricious. The settlements along the river grew slowly and the New York provincial assembly realized the need for an overland link. In 1703 they authorized the building of a road from Kingsbridge, in upper Manhattan, to Albany.

This highway came through Irvington about 1723. As traffic over it increased during the half century before the Revolution, the first foreshadowings of a village appeared as an inn became a center to serve the travelers on the road.

The tavern

[WEL]

The King's Highway was one of the main routes used by drovers. Cattle buyers purchased cattle from farmers upcountry. Drovers followed the buyers within a day or two, adding the earmarked cattle to their herds that would, at times, become obstacles on the narrow highway. At nightfall the cattle were fed and watered in fields near the inns that provided shelter and food for the drovers.

One of these inns still stands on South Broadway. Built in the 1690's as his farmhouse by Jan Harmse, the property passed to the family of Mathius Conklin after Harmse's death in 1742. A stone to the left of the front entrance (still there) is carved with the letters C, M, and S. Below the letters is the date

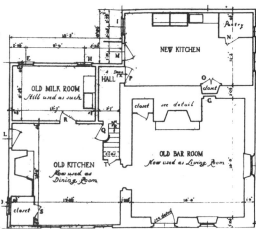

The Harmse-Odell Tavern with ground floor plan

May 8, 1746. The initials are those of Mathius and Sophia Conklin, and presumably the date records when they took possession.

Jan Harmse built his house to last. Its stone walls are two feet thick, its chestnut floor planks 2½ inches by 15 and 16 inches. Sometime after the Conklins took over the farm they made the farmhouse an inn—and tavern—as well as their family home. It became a major point of service to travelers on the King's Highway.

[WEL]

An old almanac by Nathaniel Ames of Boston, dated 1771, mentions the tavern of the Conklins as the second stop out of New York on the road to Albany and Quebec. The miles to Conklins were twenty-seven, and the number coincides roughly with the milestones twenty-six and twenty-seven that are still in place on the west side of Broad-way within the village limits. These milestone markers were placed by order of Post-master General of the Colonies, Benjamin Franklin, just prior to the Revolution.

———

After Conklin's death in 1774 the tavern came into the possession of Jonathan Odell, and it was as Odell's tavern that it was known in the period of the Revolutionary War.

No comment survives on what the Odell tavern offered a traveler of those days. The facilities were probably grim indeed by modern standards. Crowded sleeping, bedbugs, mosquitoes, washing at the pump, greasy fried food—all were common hazards of the road. On the other hand home baked bread, fresh fruit, cheeses, sweet milk and buttermilk from the spring house must have been delicacies; good ales and wines as well. Whatever the specifics the tavern must have been a

welcome haven from the boneshattering rides over the King's Highway in the crude vehicles that were the public coaches of the day.

One tavern does not make a village. But the road had called forth the tavern, that unique social stronghold of colonial times—a place to meet, to raise a glass, to eat, to spend a traveler's night, to exchange news, to discuss, to argue, to mold opinion. For the residents of what was to become Irvington, the Odell tavern must have been a window, however small, opening on the outside world.

We weighed anchor a little after six in the morning; wind southwest. . . . York island being in view at a distance. We went ashore to the house of one Kaen Buikhaut, a Dutch farmer. The old man was busy in making a slaigh, which is a travelling machine used here and at Albany in the winter time to run upon the snow. The woman told us she had eighteen children, nine boys and as many girls. Their third daughter was a handsom girl about 16 years of age. We purchased there three fat fowls for ninepence and a great bucket full of milk into the bargain.

A traveler

THE EARLY ROAD may have offered the surest speed of the day for a lone horseman, a military company, or a private carriage, but at the same time river traffic on the Hudson was increasing. Freight and travelers moved up- and downriver in a complex of winds, tides, currents, and, in season, frustrating ice.

A traveler on the river in 1744 has left a record of a stop at what was apparently the Buckhout farm in Irvington. Dr. Alexander Hamilton, no kin to his namesake, spent four days on a trip northward from New York to Albany. Southbound, what with running aground and other hazards, the time was the same.

On July 5th Dr. Hamilton arrived off what is now Irvington. His journal, published as *Gentleman's Progress*, tells of it:

Day by day

LIFE WENT ALONG on the farms that were to be Irvington, seemingly ordered and changeless in its ways, as the 18th century matured.

Even before the new century began there had been enough tenants in the manor to warrant building a church. The Old Dutch Church still stands today in North Tarrytown. Beside the door is a stone that reads: "Erected and built by Frederick Philipse and Catherine Van Cortlandt, his wife, in 1699."

[WEL]

Every able-bodied male of age was re-

14

"Sleepy Hollow" Church. North Tarrytown. Published 1867 by Currier and Ives

quired to serve in the militia, and from the beginnings farming was continually disrupted by wars and threats of wars with the French and with the Indians. During the absence of the men serving in the militia work was carried on by the young folk and the elderly. It was necessary that the land be planted, homes be kept in repair, and the rents be paid. The housewife served as midwife and doctor, concocting her own drugs and medicines from herbs and roots.

Reading a newspaper was an event. *The New York Gazette* was a weekly, first issued in 1730. Its pages were well thumbed by the time a copy traveled from the city to the Irvington vicinity. Not all the people could read. Many children never saw a school. There may have been some teaching at the church; the lucky ones had an older person at home who could teach them to read and write. Often the Bible was the only book available.

"Reading and writing and 'rithmetic..."

NOT UNTIL SOME 70 YEARS LATER was a state-wide school system established. Even then the advantages of being instructed in the three "R's" was not an unmixed boon to the young scholars. Jacob Dutcher, descendant of the early settler, Barent Dutcher, left this account of Irvington schooldays in his book *The Old Home by the River:*

The school was the most important building in the neighborhood—a familiar landmark for generations. Parents had attended it for instruction, and after them, their children.

12   13

The pretty Lambs do skip and play.

The Cat destroys the rats and mice.

The Fox conveys the fowls away.

Thy teacher gives thee good advice.

These two books belonged to Ellen Jane Mann, school-girl of Irvington, inscribed October 5, 1858

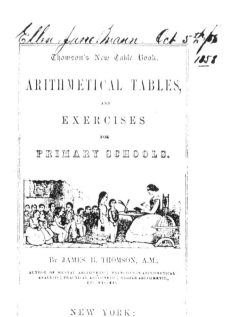

During the winter months, one evening in the week, it was used for singing school, when the young of both sexes crowded it to its utmost capacity, ostensibly for the purpose of improvement in this beautiful and useful science. These meetings, however, were rather sources of enjoyment than profit. There was more frolic than study, and more sending of love glances than attention to the rules of music.

[The schoolhouse] stood upon a knoll, a short distance from the great public thoroughfare, while another road, less travelled, crossing the first at right angles, ran along under its windows.

The building was four square. Years before it had been painted red, but the storms of winter had nearly washed its bright dress away. Underneath its narrow eaves, its boards were beautifully honeycombed by bumblebees. . . . Around three sides of the schoolroom, against the wall, were the writing desks and seats for the larger scholars. Towards the centre of the room were the low benches without backs, for the smaller children; and on these uncomfortable seats they were obliged to sit throughout the entire day.

In the middle of the floor stood the old box stove that had been used so long and so much, that it had a decidedly worn and weary look, even though it always smiled upon you through numberless cracks where the fire burned brightly. This modest little stove was expected to keep the entire room comfortable in all weathers; for the worthy trustees said that the scholars must keep themselves warm by the fires of their genius. However . . . on windy, wintry days, the currents of air from the windows, and up through the open floor, materially modified the heat from the little box stove, and altogether extinguished the fires of genius.

Against the wall stood the Master's desk, facing the scholars. Against one wall leaned a ladder to a small dark room above known as the "dungeon." . . .

No greater or more dreaded punishment could be inflicted than to be shut up in this dungeon. Mice, even during school hours, held high carnival there. According to the belief of the boys, it was peopled with all manner of terrible things. Even now, I can see the imploring look, and hear the entreaty, not to be shut in the *dungeon*. But these appeals were seldom heeded; and many an unfortunate young culprit was shut in there, for a season, away from the outer world, almost in total darkness.

Yet the scholars had their fun.

At no great distance from the school were pleasant woods in which to ramble; and nearer still, its brook in which to play. In it we constructed our pond. Our miniature ships floated upon its surface, and our thoughts were drawn toward it during our hours of study.

Schoolboys handed down the legend of graves and ghostly presences beneath the old schoolhouse on the hill where some heroic American soldiers of the Revolution, basely shot by Tories, had been buried before the schoolhouse was built. Any boy daring to crawl into the dimly-lit graveyard under the building was a hero in his own right.

The rising wind

AFTER 1750 the distinctively Dutch character of the residents began to alter as settlers of other national origins, mostly English, came into the area. The Hudson River country felt the impact.

[WEL]

Traffic on the Hudson River increased. Sloops carried pioneer families, their domestic animals and implements to the north. The vast forest of virgin pines began to appear in the form of rafts along the river, guided by crews known as "tiders." The great local forest had disappeared west of the highway and only wood lots and pasture lands existed along the higher land to the east.

An early Hudson River sloop

American Revolutionary soldiers at musket drill

Fields of wheat, corn and oats supplied the family larder, and the surplus became the cargo of the local market sloops bound for New York City.

But the most important changes were forging a new country. English and colonial arms broke French control to the north, and all eastern North America seemed securely English. But a wind was rising. Throughout the colonies confidence and energy skyrocketed, restlessness took root against restrictions and controls from across the sea. Fighting with British troops flared at Lexington and Concord, and the colonies moved uncertainly into rebellion. Purposes hardened, and rebellion became revolution.

Revolution

WHEN REVOLUTION CAME, no less an authority than John Adams estimated that one-third of the colonists wanted independence, one-third wanted to remain loyal to England, and one-third was totally indifferent. But the times forced decision, and decision must have been agonizing for the great landlords of New York. The lord of Philipse Manor vacillated, and remained a loyalist. For his tenants too it was a time of decision. One hundred and sixty-three of them tell the story in the course of a petition they sent to the New York legislature in 1779:

It is well known to several members of your honorable houses that our landlord in the first of these troubles, espoused our cause, but soon after sent up a writing purporting a protest against Congresses and Committees, which he enjoined us, the inhabitants, to sign, or we should labor under his displeasure; but disregarding his threats the inhabitants had a meeting and concluded not to sign the paper; and not long after we were all summoned to meet Mr. Philipse at the White Plains, expecting by his presence to awe his tenants into compliance, but to his mortification found we had virtue enough (a few only excepted) to refuse him, being not only then determined to risk all properties in the glorious cause of Liberty, and are still fixed in our resolutions to persevere to the end of the contest.

By late summer of 1776 the war came to Westchester and the farms of Irvington.

In July the British landed an army—32,000 men—on Staten Island in a cautious advance against New York. George Washington moved his troops to Long Island, and waited. Late in August the attack came. For the Americans the battle was a disaster in dead and wounded and prisoners. Throughout one black, rainy night, unit by unit, the Americans retreated over Brooklyn Heights. Guides passed them along in the darkness, and silent boat crews rowed and sailed them across the East River to Manhattan and safety.

It was at Odell's tavern in Irvington that the newly-created State of New York received the official report that Washington had lost Long Island. The Committee of Safety, the legislature's executive committee, met at Odell's on August 31st. The Committee received Washington's report and drafted an appropriate reply, then went on to such routine matters as providing for employment of Long Island militiamen who had been driven from their homes.

To Irvington's farmers the war came with a vengeance. A detachment of British troops under General Vaughan camped on the Odell and Buckhout farms on high ground west of Broadway.

William Dutcher, who was already serving as a captain in the militia, moved his family north for refuge with relatives in Salem, leaving his farm in the care of his Negro slaves.

Captain Buckhout, then a venerable 94, fought a plundering sailor from a British ship and was stabbed. English authorities sentenced the sailor to prison, and Captain Buckhout survived to live on to 103.

British soldiers were living off the land. Jonathan Odell's orchard and fences went for firewood. About 1000 bushels of wheat in the sheaf were destroyed, and his hogs were butchered for meat.

Neutral ground

THE PATRIOTS controlled northern Westchester. The British and the Tories who had fled as refugees to English protection commanded the southern part of the county. Between the two lay the "neutral ground," controlled by neither. Irvington was in the heart of the neutral ground.

Throughout the war troops from both sides moved through the Irvington area on swift probing raids. Bitterness between former neighbors became hatred. Tories, clinging to old loyalties, lost the livelihoods and lands they felt were rightfully theirs, and hatred became cruelty on both sides. The settled and comfortable pattern of farm life eroded, and once prosperous farmers struggled to exist. Marauding bands of thieves scourged the countryside—the Cowboys, ostensibly loyalist, and the Skinners American.

Washington Irving noted: ". . . [Skinners and Loyalists], in the hurry of their military ardor, were apt to err on the safe side, and rob friend as well as foe. Neither of them stopped to ask the politics of horse or cow, which they drove into captivity; nor, when they wrung the neck of a rooster, did they trouble their heads to ascertain whether he were crowing for Congress or for King George."

Three times hanged—and saved. Caesar lived but a neighbor, Polly Buckhout, fared less well. Wearing a man's hat, her sex was mistaken by a British soldier who shot and killed her.

Rescue

A GROUP OF HESSIANS raided the Odell farm for food. Violence was no respecter of status. The soldiers seized a Negro slave, Caesar. He refused to tell where the food supply was hidden. They led him to a tree and hanged him. They cut him down. He still refused to tell. Again they hanged him, and cut him down, and again he would not tell.

They hanged him a third time and rode off. A family account says that two girls of the household rushed to the rescue. One girl knelt while the other climbed on her back to cut the rope.

A raiding party from a British ship partially burned the Ecker house, later to become Washington Irving's Sunnyside, and the Van Tassels, Ecker relatives who were then living there, had to flee into the winter's cold, saving only the clothes they were wearing.

When General Vaughan's troops moved onto the Odell place Jonathan Odell and four other men from the neighborhood were seized and imprisoned in the Old Dutch Church in New York. Jonathan Odell survived prison and war to drive his gig with its brightly painted wheels up to the Old Dutch Church on Sundays.

Escape

BY THE WINTER of 1777–1778 the Dutchers had returned from northern Westchester. Captain Dutcher was away, serving in the army, but Mrs. Dutcher has left an account of a raid on her home:

My husband was serving in the American army as Captain, and having been a long time away from us, he obtained permission from his commanding officer to accompany a detachment on its secret mission [in the Irvington area] that he might make a brief visit home. He reached the house one day just before sunset. I remember, when he entered, his coming was so unexpected. We were so happy that we gathered around him, laughing and crying by turns. Very thankfully and joyfully that day, we sat down to our evening meal. When he left us, the uncertainties of the war were so great that we did not know whether we should ever see him again. Besides some of the Tories with whom he had previously been acquainted were determined to kill him.

Our meal was ended when night fairly set in. The sky, however, being cloudless, the moon at its full, and the ground covered with snow, it was sufficiently light to see objects at a great distance. We were about rising from the table, when our attention was suddenly attracted by one of the children who was standing at the window, as she said, "Oh father, yonder are some soldiers coming this way." A single glance in the direction in which she was pointing showed that they were Tories.

Not a moment must be lost if he would escape. Snatching up his hat and sword, my husband left the house by a door opposite to the one they were about to enter, well knowing his fate should he fall into their hands. Fortunately, before he came into the house, he had fed and secured his horse in a spot some distance away, and quite hidden from view. Could he keep the dwelling between his pursuers and himself till he reached this place he would be in comparative safety, at least he would have time to mount, and his chances of escape would be better on horseback than on foot.

It could not have been more than a moment after I had seen him disappear than the door shook beneath the heavy blows of sabres. My children clung to me, though I was trembling with fear. For their sake, I assumed a courage I did not feel. I had hardly removed the last bar, when the door was thrown violently open, and six rough, powerful, and evil-looking men stood before me.

"Where is your rebel husband?" demanded the leader.

Striving to be calm, I answered, "He is not in the house."

"I do not believe you. If we find him I will hang him before your eyes."

Then turning to his men he ordered them, with a savage oath, to search in every corner. This they did, and in doing it destroyed everything that came in their way. They spared nothing. Seeing his men returning alone the leader became furious.

"Where is the cursed rebel?"

"I cannot tell you."

"If he is gone, which way did he go? If you do not tell me, I will drag you from the house, and tie you to one of these trees to freeze."

I do not know to what length he would have gone had not a guard outside called loudly, "There goes the rebel," and fired.

It was as I expected. The road around the dwelling described almost a semicircle; and, though in places partially hidden from view, there was one spot entirely exposed. Could he pass that place without detection he might escape. He was passing over that part, when a neigh from the Tory's horse caused the rider to look up and follow the direction of the animal's gaze. At once he recognized the fugitive. At the same moment he shouted and discharged his pistol. Fortunately his aim was so quick that it was untrue.

By this time my husband had passed the place, and an open path lay before him. The leader, in excited tones, ordered his men to mount and pursue. And only waiting long enough to hurl the most awful curses upon me and upon all patriots, followed, and the race for life began. For some distance the inclination of the road was such that by stepping a few yards from the house we could command a view of the parties.

I knew that my husband's horse was a hardy, swift animal, and was therefore perplexed and troubled to see the others gain on him. The cause was soon apparent. The pursuers in their eagerness to take him dead or alive, had discharged their pieces at random; and before giving them time to reload, he slackened his horse's speed, and drawing his pistols from their holsters, took deliberate aim at the two foremost, and fired in quick succession. Both reeled in their saddles, and for a moment it was doubtful whether they could retain their seats.

Profiting by the confusion into which they were thrown, the rebel, as they called my

Eager to take him dead or alive

husband, put spurs to his horse and again they began that fearful ride. They soon passed entirely from sight; but now and then a loud shout, and an occasional report, that was borne with great distinctness upon the frosty night air, assured me that the race was still kept up. They pressed him so hard that his horse began to show signs of weariness. And when he at length rode into camp, worn out himself, his poor tired beast, though the night was intensely cold, was covered with foam.

Petticoat Lane

IRVINGTON'S FARMS sent others to give solid service to their new country. Ecker-Acker, Van Tassel, Dutcher, Jewell, Odell—the roster of names is familiar to Irvington.

John Odell was about twenty years old when the war began, one of three brothers who were to serve. He seemed to have an extraordinary affinity for trouble at a time when trouble was not hard to come by.

In addition to fighting in the Mohawk Valley, John served as one of the key men fighting the small battles of a guerrilla war that swept over the neutral ground for seven years.

He was the senior guide when George Washington's army marched out of northern Westchester and down the Saw Mill River valley in July of 1781 to join with the French in the hills back of Dobbs Ferry on the way to Yorktown.

Along with the founding fathers John may have pledged his life, his fortune, his sacred honor, but he also ran into some confusion with his trousers. At one point he heard that a group of Tories or Cowboys had taken possession of the McCormick house about a mile west of Elmsford on the White Plains Road from Tarrytown. He quickly brought together a small force and drove them out. Wisely enough he stayed on for the night, and had to repel a surprise counter attack. Daylight came with a relief force but somewhere in the line of duty John's trousers were missing. He had no choice. He borrowed a skirt from the lady of the house and rode out to meet his colonel. The laugh echoed around the farms, and until the joke was old and memory faded, White Plains Road out of Tarrytown was known as Petticoat Lane.

The British offered 100 pounds reward for John Odell, but his gray horse that Colonel Van Cortlandt had presented to him was one of the fastest and most dashing in the County.

A final note for John Odell. In 1782 he was on a visit to his sweetheart, Hannah McChain, near Tarrytown, when a raiding party of Tories struck. Hannah saw them coming and rushed John to the garret. He stretched out on a plank in a dark section under the roof and waited out the search. Hannah hid him well. They did not find him. The account concludes: "The following year, peace having been declared they were married."

Aftermath

THE WAR left a ravaged countryside. A traveler who was there and saw it has left this account:

The country is rich and fertile, and the farms appear to have been advantageously

24

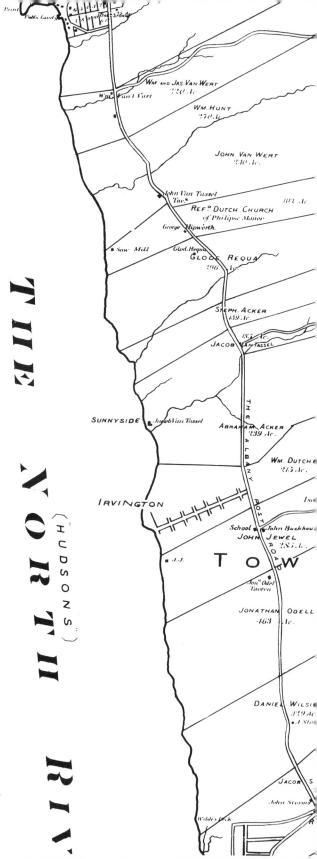

cultivated, but it now has the marks of a country in ruins, a large portion of the proprietors having abandoned their homes. The few that remain have found it impossible to harvest the crops.

On the high roads where heretofore was a continuous stream of travelers and vehicles, not a single traveler was seen from week to week, month to month. The country-side was silent.

The very tracks of the carriages were grown over with grass or weeds. Travelers walked along bypaths. The villages are abandoned, the residents having fled to the north, leaving their homes, where possible, in charge of elder persons and servants.

A different drum

To THE TORY LORD of the manor, Frederick Philipse, the end of the war brought confiscation of his lands by the State of New York. For his tenants in as yet unborn Irvington— Abraham Ecker, William Dutcher, John Jewell, Jonathan Odell—it was an opportunity

Detail from Map of Manor of Philipsburgh, 1785. Prepared for the Commissioners of Forfeitures. Traced and reduced, with additions, by M. K. Couzens in 1880

25

Commercial Mail Stage 1815

to buy at auction outright ownership of the lands their families had farmed for almost a hundred years—lands that comprised the main portion of the nearly 2000 acres that now are included within the present village of Irvington.

Once more cattle on the way to market clogged Broadway. The new Acker Inn, a half mile north of Odell's, was a popular stop with the drovers. But the inn had more notable guests as well. Its registers contain the names of Alexander Hamilton, Aaron Burr, Jerome Bonaparte, Napoleon's brother.

Public stage wagons made regular trips between New York and Albany, with Odell's Inn once more an overnight stop. The transportation company's charter, granted by the New York legislature, required the company to supply two wagons with sheltering covers against rain, snow, and sun, to be drawn by four able horses, a trip to be made at least once a week in each direction at a fare of three cents a mile.

[WEL]

Try to visualize the Post Road through Irvington about 1815. It was just wide enough for two wagons to pass. It was bordered with grass plots where black-eyed Susans, daisies, and buttercups grew in season. A rough stone wall on each side of the road prevented the drovers' cattle from wandering into the grain fields.

———

The War of 1812 brought echoes of the Revolution to Irvington. Sons and grandsons of the old veterans went to war.

A troop of cavalry from Kentucky displaced the cattle at the Acker Inn on the Post Road, and officers' signatures filled the tavern guest book.

North to the West

ONE QUIET AUGUST AFTERNOON in 1807 Robert Fulton's *Clermont* chugged past Irvington on its way up the Hudson River (thirty-two hours from New York to Albany) and left in its sturdy wake a change in American life. The age of steamboats on the rivers was born. When the Erie Canal opened in 1825 the Hudson River became a part of the great new waterway to the west. A flow of ships bore a moving tapestry of passengers and freight up and down the Hudson. Settlers, with all their goods, headed for new land along the Great Lakes.

The new commerce had a sharp effect on Irvington.

[WEL]

The price of local crops declined steadily. The bellowing of cattle and the crowing fowl in the pens aboard the sloops on the river were answered by those on the river's shore with resounding effect on the pocket-books of Irvington's farmers.

But if the Lord took away He also gave. A boon came from another source. Irvington's rolling acres along the river became a haven for wealthy New York City residents escaping the city's fires and fever epidemics.

Wolfert's Roost

EARLIER, IN 1812, Justus Dearman had bought land from the estate of William Dutcher II. By chance and in time it became the center of the village. Briefly the village

Fulton's Folly, the "Clermont", entering the Tappan Zee

Washington Irving, age 26.
Painting by John Wesley
Jarvis

Washington Irving, age 76.
Photograph by Mathew Brady

Wolfert's Roost "Purchased by Washington Irving, Esq. to improve for a Summer
Residence"

took its name from him—*Dearman*—but another name was waiting—*Irvington*.

In 1835 Washington Irving bought a part of the Ecker farm, including the original farmhouse, adjoining land that his nephew Oscar Irving had bought fourteen years earlier.

Washington Irving described it: "It is a beautiful spot, capable of being made a little paradise. There is a small Dutch cottage on it that was built about a century since and inhabited by one of the Van Tassel family. I have had an architect there, and shall build a mansion upon the place this summer. My idea is to make a little nookery, somewhat in the Dutch style, quaint but unpretending."

This was Wolfert's Roost, later called Sunnyside.

Years later Jennie Black recalled a visit to Irving's home:

I think one of my most treasured memories of extreme youth was the day my dear mother took me to call on the Misses Irving at Sunnyside. For years I had spent much of my time in the woods and the lane leading to Irving's home. I had paddled in the

. . . *later Sunnyside*

brook, hunted chestnuts in the fall and played by the hour in a great tree by the side of the brook.

Sunnyside, in those days, was unchanged from the time when Irving had lived there —the north wing not having been built until years later. His library was on the right as one entered, the formal parlor on the left; back of this the living-room, with its French doors opening out to the west porch. To this room we were ushered.

After waiting a short time, only one of the Misses Irving entered the room, explaining

Irving at one time used his study and library alcove as sleeping quarters

The Headless Horseman by William J. Wilgus. The climactic moment in Irving's story of Ichabod Crane

that the intense heat had given her sister a headache and she begged to be excused. These two ladies were Mr. Irving's nieces, and were living with him when he passed away in 1859. I wish that I might paint Miss Irving as I saw her. Rather short, with dark curls on either side of a small oval face, hair parted in the center and eyes that

The Return of Rip Van Winkle. A painting of Irving's famous character by John Quidor

made one wonder, their expression was so soft—so wistful. She told us that the sisters feared to remain there because of their remoteness from any neighbors. At that time there were no houses to be seen from the lane. The railroad, just below the house, was infested with tramps, who often alarmed them. Even as she spoke, a horrid hairy-faced figure appeared at the open French window leading to the porch. Stepping lightly toward the window, in a frightened, timid voice she said: "Go away, go away, this is a private house." And he went with surprising agility. I was greatly relieved. "That is why sister and I cannot stay in this lovely place," she explained, as she resumed her seat.

Tea was served.

About the same time that Washington Irving bought Wolfert's Roost James Hamilton, a son of Alexander Hamilton, acquired a substantial neighboring estate. He took Ir-

30

Colonel Hamilton's Nevis

ving's suggestion and named it Nevis for the West Indies island where his father had been born.

A letter written by Edward Jaffray, Irving's neighbor, describes how the Irvington countryside looked from the opposite shore of the Hudson.

"In the year 1849 I hired a house at Nyack for the summer, and in the afternoons we used to sit on the piazza and look across the river. We used to remark how few country seats there were, and how bare of trees the greatest part of the land was. When Colonel Hamilton built his house, in 1836, there was but *one* tree on the entire plot of ground."

Hamilton, then in his late forties, had been a successful lawyer, a Manhattan real estate investor, soldier in the War of 1812, and for a time acting Secretary of State under President Andrew Jackson. He took his new role of country gentleman seriously, even to the extent of making a trip to Europe to study agricultural methods. He brought back valuable information, a bull and two cows of Durham stock, a pair of terrier dogs for use against the rats, and a Scottish gardener.

The Tappan Sea, 1820. The general area of Irvington lies between Dobbs Ferry and the Pennybridge brook, just north of the C. Pindar farm

The happy scar

NEW YORK CITY still needed water. A dam built on the Croton River fed its water some thirty miles to the city. The aqueduct that carried it passed through Irvington.

To generations in Irvington the old Croton Aqueduct has been almost a symbol of a quiet, long-ago, rural past.

[WEL]

The walk along this old aqueduct has long been a favorite pastime for the residents in this area. I once counted thirty-three different varieties of trees as I walked along its almost two miles of splendor. The same day I saw tracks in the snow of fox, raccoon, rabbit, and not far away possum and muskrat.

Deer, and even skunks, might have been added to the list.

The aqueduct was a raw gash across the farm lands. Everything that crossed it had to be accommodated to it. Brooks were led under it. In places old farm roads had to change course, swinging to run parallel until they could turn and make a crossing.

The men who built the aqueduct were a brawling camp of fighters who easily evaded the contractors' best efforts to keep them and whiskey apart. A strike in 1839 ended in a drunken uproar, with one man left dead. A year later more violence led the Governor to call out the militia.

The aqueduct measured 7'8" wide and 8'5½" high. In construction it was an inverted horseshoe in shape with its top arched by brick and its walls of 4½" stone set in

Below, building the sidewalls of the Aqueduct. The Aqueduct was re-opened (right) and put to new use in 1971, converted from one necessity to another. It now houses telephone and electric power cables underground

Rosedale cement. The stone for Irvington's part of the aqueduct was blasted and dug from a quarry near the Presbyterian Church. The quarry was filled in long ago and now lies under the bowling green behind the church.

On a bright morning in June 1842, members of the New York City Board of Water Commissioners began a walk by lantern light through the thirty-three-mile length of the aqueduct from the dam to the Harlem River to make a final inspection. They reached Irvington by nightfall. After a night's rest at Acker's Inn they proceeded on their way and reached the Harlem River late in the afternoon of June 9.

There was a more unofficial inspection. Two weeks later when the first few inches of water were being sent through the tunnel four hardy pioneers floated down the aqueduct in a flat-bottomed vessel christened the *Croton Maid*.

The first water to be distributed from the aqueduct reached New York City on October 14, 1842. The vision, the planning, the work, the brawling—all the forces that created the aqueduct are long gone, but they left a beautiful path, a happy scar.

Voyage of the "Croton Maid"

Rails along the river

THE FIRST RAILROAD along the Hudson was the Erie, on its western shore. The terminal of its tracks, the Long Dock, jutting out almost a mile from the Hudson's bank to reach deep water, was directly opposite Irvington.

[WEL]

The paddle wheels of the *New Haven,* the *Francis Sciddy,* the *Thomas Powell,* and the ironclad *Erie* churned the river from the Long Dock to New York carrying passengers, grain, fruit, potatoes from the west, and milk and poultry from the local farms. Back up the river from the city came the hardware, cloth, shoes, a thousand items headed westward for the farms.

When the winter's ice interrupted service on the river, passengers were transported by horsedrawn sleighs across to the east shore of the river where they trudged up the ferry road in Irvington to meet the stage on the Post Road and complete their journey.

Except when the river was frozen over a ferry service was provided by Ben Jewell from the Long Dock to the foot of the ferry road in Irvington, a road running along the dividing line between the old Dutcher and Dearman farms up the hill to the Post Road. Cattle from the Erie's western trains crowded the ferry and jammed between the stone fences of the ferry road in the laborious climb up the hill to pasture in the fields near the Acker Inn.

The no longer quiet "Nookery"

IRVINGTON · 1852

By 1849 the railroad moved up the Hudson's eastern shore and invaded Irvington. "The abominable screeching of the locomotive," Washington Irving called it from his no longer quiet "nookery."

The railroad project was not without opposition on the ground that it would mar the beauty of the Hudson Valley. In answer to this objection John B. Jarvis, the engineer who surveyed and laid out the right of way, made a notable statement:

"To a very great extent the construction of the road will improve the shore, rough points will be smoothed off, the irregular indentation of the bays will be hidden and regularity

New York Central and Hudson River Railroad Timetable 1885. Early fare from New York to Yonkers was 25 cents. The fare has increased but the running time has not noticeably improved

Rhinebeck										27	8 12																						7 26	
Staatsburgh		Do									8 22																						7 35	
Hyde Park											8 30																						7 35	
Poughkeepsie	4 40	5 10			6 25		5		9 00	9 05	10 10	12 10	1 05		4 50	4 33					7 21	7 55												
Milton Ferry					6 32					9 21	10 26		1 22		4 38																			
New Hamburgh					6 42	7 29				9 21	10 26		1 22		4 47							8 12												
Low Point					6 46										4 52																			
Fishkill		5 37			6 54	7 41			S	9 43	103	12 34	1 34		5 15	5 09					7 46	8 24												
Dutch. & Col. Junc.										9 36						5 03																		
Cornwall				7 47						9 40			1 41			5 07																		
Cold Spring				7 08	7 54					9 47			1 47			5 11					8 37													
Garrisons				7 14	8 00				9 36	9 53	10 53	12 47	1 53		5 30	5 35					8 43													
Highlands				7 21												5 42					8 51													
Peekskill		6 10		7 00	7 33	8 15		8 35	S	10 11	11 11	11 20	2 12	3 00		5 52					9 02													
Montrose				7 05	7 38			8 41				11 25		3 05		5 58																		
Crugers				7 09				8 45				11 29		3 08		6 01																		
Oscawana				7 12				8 48				11 32				6 04																		
Croton		6 00		6 40	7 00	7 16	7 45	8 00	8 31	8 52	10 35	11 36	1 27	2 30	3 15	4 10	5 30		6 08	6 25	7 30				8 45	9 30								
Sing Sing		6 05	6 30	6 46	7 00	7 25	7 54	8 06	8 32	8 37	9 00	10 39	10 41	11 45	1 31	2 30	2 36	3 25	4 16	5 36	6 17	6 31	7 36	9 24	8 51	9 36								
Scarborough		6 10		6 50	7 10	7 29	7 57	8 10	8 40	9 03	10 45	11 49	2 40	3 29	4 21	5 40		6 21	6 35	7 40			8 55	9 40										
Tarrytown		6 17		6 57	7 17	7 37	8 06	8 17	S	8 47	9 12	10 41	10 52	11 57	1 42	2 41	2 47	3 37	4 27	5 47	6 28	6 56	7 47	9 36	9 0	9 47								
Irvington		6 23		7 02	7 22	7 42	8 11	8 22	8 52	9 17	10 57	12 02	1 47	2 52	3 41	4 32	5 52		7 00	7 52	9 07	9 52												
Dobb's Ferry		6 27		7 07	7 27	7 48	8 17	8 27	4 57	9 23	11 02	12 09	1 52	1 57	3 48	4 37	5 57		7 05	7 57	9 12	9 57												
Hastings		6 30		7 10	7 30	7 52	8 20	8 30	9 00	9 27	11 05	12 13	1 55	3 00	3 52	4 40	6 01		7 08	8 00	9 15	10 00												
Glenwood		6 36		7 16	7 36	7 59	8 36		9 06	9 32	11 11	12 20	2 01	3 06	4 46	6 06		7 14	8 06	9 21	10 06													
Yonkers	6 28	6 39		7 19	7 39	8 02	8 30	8 40	9 09	9 37	11 00	11 14	12 22	2 04	3 00	3 09	4 01	4 43	6 03	6 48	7 16	8 09	8 52	9 57	9 24	10 09								
Ludlow		6 42		7 22	7 42		8 43		9 12	9 39	11 17	12 24	2 07	3 12	4 52	6 12		7 18	8 12	9 27	10 12													
Mt. St. Vincent		6 44		7 24	7 44		8 45		9 14	9 42	11 19	12 25	2 09	3 14	4 05	4 54	6 14		7 20	8 14	9 29	10 14												
Riverdale		6 46		7 26	7 46	8 08	8 47		9 16	9 45	11 21	12 28	2 11	3 16	4 08	4 56	6 16		7 22	8 16	9 31	10 16												
Spuyten Duyvil		6 50		7 29	7 50	8 12	8 50		9 19	9 47	11 25	12 32	2 15	3 20	4 12	5 00	6 20		7 25	8 20	9 35	10 20												
Kings Bridge		6 54			7 54		8 54		S	9 51	11 29	12 36	2 19	3 24	5 01	6 24		7 29	8 21	9 39	10 24													
Morris Dock		6 58			7 58		8 58		S	9 54	11 33	12 39	2 23	3 28	5 08	6 28		7 33	8 28	9 41	10 28													
High Bridge		7 01		8 01			9 01		S	9 57	11 36	12 42	2 26	3 31	S	5 11	6 31		7 36	8 31	9 46	10 31												
Harlem (125th St.)		7 07		8 07				S					2 32	3 20	4 27	6 37	7 12		9 12	10 22	10 37													
G'd Cen'l Depot.	7 00	7 15	7 30	7 50	8 15	8 35	9 00	9 15	9 20	10 15	11 00	11 33	11 50	12 25	1 00	2 12	2 40	3 28	3 45	4 35	5 25	6 45	7 00	7 20	7 50	8 45	9 20	10 30	10 00	10 45				
NEW YORK	AM	AM	AM	AM	AM	AM	AM	AM	AM	AM	AM	AM	AM	PM	PM	PM	PM	PM	PM	PM	PM	PM	PM	PM	PM	PM	PM	PM	PM	PM				

and symmetry imparted to the outline of the shore, thus by a combination of the works of nature and of art, adding to the interest, grandeur and beauty of the whole."

America was building railroads, and certainly beauty was not about to stand in the way.

[WEL]

The first train on a regular run chuffed into Irvington on September 29, 1849, its passengers from Peekskill to Chambers Street paying fifty cents for the trip. Service consisted of four passenger trains and one freight train each way every day. The railroad remained single track until expansion began when the road was completed through to Albany in 1851.

For Irvington by 1850 the past was gone beyond recall. An extraordinarily able group of businessmen, political figures, and professional men were moving from New York City onto the farmland acres, and building their houses with a peculiar mystique of simplicity and ornateness. The views of the river were magnificent. Gardeners, groundkeepers, grooms, and liverymen came to care for the new estates.

Almost belatedly a village center was born.

Village Lots and Cottage Sites at
DEARMAN, WLSTCHESTER C?.
adjacent to the
Hudson River Station & Piermont Ferry Depot

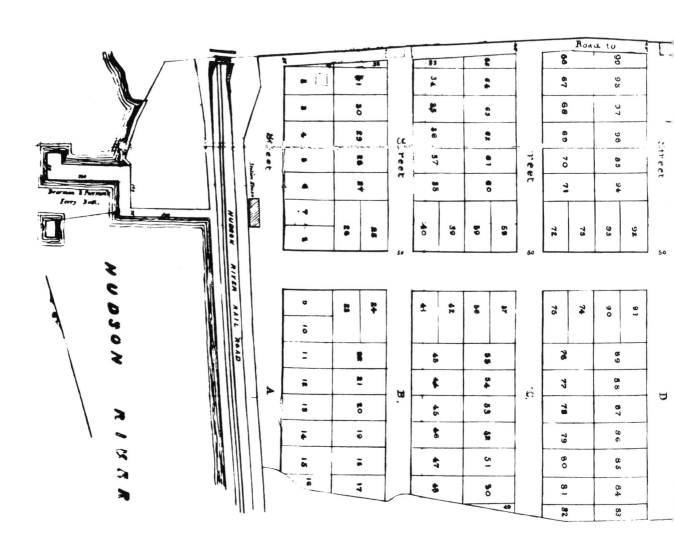

to be sold at auction by —

Cole & Chilton

on Thursday 25.th April 1850 at 12 o'clock, at the

Merchants' Exchange N.Y.

Miller's Lith 101 Broadway NY

Scale 100 feet per Inch

Dimensions of full Lots 50 by 100 Feet.

Railway   Bridge & Ferry

Avenue   70 feet wide

E.   F.   G.   Aqueduct   H.

Street   Street   Street

Note. These premises rise in an even and gentle slope from the river to the Turnpike Road, commanding an extensive and beautiful view up & down the Hudson from far above Sing Sing to Staten Island and the Narrows.

37

Birth
of a village

LATE IN THE FALL of 1849 two deeds were recorded that transferred to Franklin C. Field the farmland property of Justus Dearman.

Mr. Field had the old farm surveyed and laid out into streets and 266 building lots extending eastward from the river. The lots were auctioned at the Merchants Exchange in New York City on Monday, April 25, 1850. [WEL]

In a year's time a reporter for a New York newspaper described the scene: "It all seems like magic. In so short a time the germ of a beautiful village is producing new neighbors for Sunnyside. A main street has been laid out, and side streets run north and south, much like the arms of telegraph poles. The depot at the foot of the Main Avenue is the most picturesque of station houses on the Hudson River Railroad.

The new village center prospered. A map dated 1851 showed a cluster of buildings near the railroad station. They included a general store and post office, a small hotel and a coal and lumber yard.

About the same time the lots of the village were sold another development, centered in East and West Clinton Avenues, was brought to the auction rooms. This was Abbotsford. It was not destined to have an independent existence, but was to merge into Irvington.

In the immediate area of Abbotsford another property was sold. The so-called "mansion house," built on the heart of the old Odell farm, became the attractive center of an estate, a property that included the Odell homestead, the tavern.

The place caught the eye of one of the

Opposite the depot, circa 1860

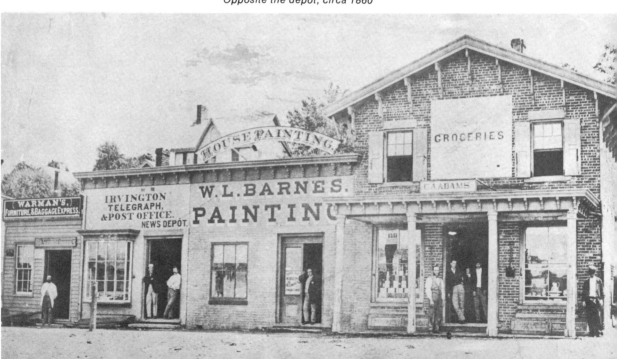

Opposite the depot—thirty years later

hard-driving businessmen who were making New York the nation's greatest commercial city. The buyer was John Gottlieb Wendel. He had emigrated from Germany in 1798 as a boy and in 1822 he married Elizabeth Astor. Like his brother-in-law, John Jacob Astor, he distrusted banks. Lot by lot he pursued his growing fortune up Manhattan Island.

John Wendel's son fathered a son and several daughters. Only one of the children, a daughter, married, and that marriage was childless. John Gottlieb Wendel II ruled the family with an iron hand.

The Wendels' mansion house stood high on a knoll on the west side of Broadway, near the old Odell tavern, and it was the family's

Abbotsford Hotel, a famous tavern of its day. It was eventually bought by the eccentric Miss Ella Wendel—to be torn down

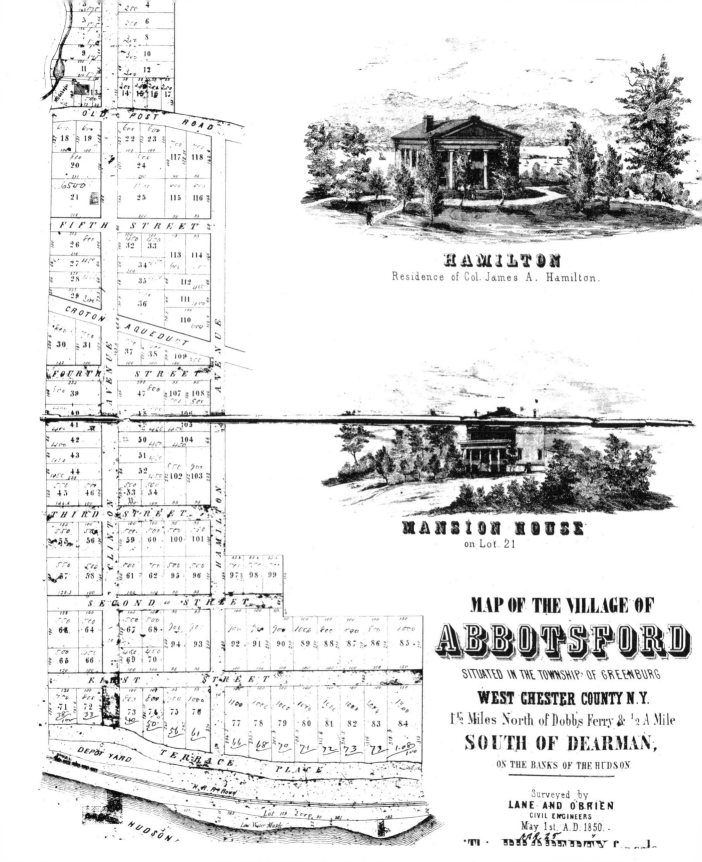

HAMILTON

Residence of Col. James A. Hamilton.

MANSION HOUSE

on Lot 21

MAP OF THE VILLAGE OF
ABBOTSFORD

SITUATED IN THE TOWNSHIP OF GREENBURG

WEST CHESTER COUNTY N.Y.

1½ Miles North of Dobb's Ferry & ½ A Mile

SOUTH OF DEARMAN,

ON THE BANKS OF THE HUDSON

Surveyed by

LANE AND O'BRIEN

CIVIL ENGINEERS

May 1st A.D. 1850.

summer home for eighty years. Foursquare, built of stone, without the nonsense of shrubbery, it was a fitting home for its owners. Jennie Black remembers them coming into the Presbyterian Church of a Sunday:

The five Wendel sisters and their brother all looked so funny, the sisters as they all seemed to dress alike with sailor hats with black elastic bands under their chins; the brother, with black wavy hair and curly mustache, who sat at the end of the pew, reminded me of a wooden mannequin. I had often watched this Wendel family group when I sat in our family pew. They were so unreal. They never moved or spoke and filed in and out of the church like so many automatons.

The Wendel fortune grew into one of the country's greatest. As the years went by and the daughters aged, the family became more dour and more recessive.

Finally only Miss Ella Wendel was left, withdrawn and eccentric. For years she drove behind a spanking team of horses, her groom seated by her side. When the horses died she refused to replace them or use any other transportation. No car was allowed inside her gates. Callers had to alight on Broadway and walk to her door, and she herself always walked.

Miss Ella's affection for her little dog, Toby, was legendary. A neighbor met her one day and found her obviously upset be-

The Wendel House, cloistered and shuttered, from which only one sister escaped to marry

One of the last Wendel coachmen

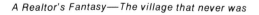

A Realtor's Fantasy—The village that never was

Miss Ella von E. Wendel and Toby

41

cause Toby was limping. The neighbor took a stone from Toby's paw and made bold to suggest that if Miss Wendel would have her driveway cemented there would be no more stones to cause such catastrophes. Nothing was too good for Toby. The driveway was paved.

François and Madame Cottenet

The inner circle

IF MR. WENDEL LOOKED ABOUT him when he arrived at Dearman-Abbotsford he would have seen exceptional neighbors. They were men of broad interests—business, political, and literary. At the heart of the group was Washington Irving. He was at the height of his fame, but it was his rare gift for friendship that warmed the circle.

A few stand out from the group. James Hamilton of Nevis, Irving's close friend for twenty-five years, had a flair for action, a temperament for battle, totally different from Irving's instinct for expression. Like or unlike, the friendship prospered.

Another member of the group, living just south of Nevis, was François Cottenet, a Frenchman who had established a highly successful importing business in New York City. In 1852–53 he built his house, which still stands. Its buff stones were quarried in

France at Nuits on the Côte d'Or, where Cottenet was born. The stones were cut to specification and brought across the Atlantic as ballast in Cottenet's sailing ships. Unloaded at Dobbs Ferry, they were hauled by oxen to the building site. The house became one of the show places in Westchester County.

Cottenet occupied his house until 1884. In the following years it had distinguished owners—Cyrus Field, John Jacob Astor III, and Amzi L. Barber, who was known as the "Asphalt King."

Next to Sunnyside to the north lived Moses Grinnell, a nephew of Irving's by marriage. His firm of Grinnell and Minturn was one of the largest suppliers of produce and staples to New York City's retail markets. The famous clipper ship "Flying Cloud" proudly carried his house flag. A successful politician, his political contacts were wide. On occasion he used them skillfully for Irving. An adroit turn of conversation at a dinner with Daniel Webster, Secretary of State, and Irving became Minister to Spain.

A neighbor who was a particularly close friend of Irving was George Morgan, a

Cyrus W. Field who laid the first Atlantic cable

"Nuits" the Cottenet home later owned by John Jacob Astor, Cyrus Field, Chauncey Depew, Amzi L. Barber

John Jacob Astor. When he lived in Irvington he built stone pillars, which still stand, at the Broadway entrance to his estate. They were known as "The Pearly Gates"

June Wedding, Ardsley Towers, 1897. The bride was Amzi Lorenzo Barber's daughter Lorena who married Samuel Davis

George D. Morgan's Woodcliff. The younger J. P. Morgan was born here unexpectedly while his parents were making a Sunday visit

nephew of Edwin Morgan, past president of the New York and Hudson Railroad and former Governor of New York. George Morgan was a brother of J. P. Morgan, Sr., and one of the founders of the banking House of Morgan. More than anyone else he worked behind the scenes to change the village name from Dearman to Irvington.

Like so many others of Irving's neighbors, Edward Jaffray was an exceptionally successful merchant in New York City who had made Irvington his summer home.

Jaffray tells about his first contacts with Irving:

Washington Irving called at my house and welcomed me and my family to the neighborhood. We found him a most genial and entertaining companion, and from that period until his death we saw him almost daily. He would frequently come up the lane to our house in the evening, sometimes alone, sometimes accompanied by one or more of his nieces, who made their home with him.

He was very fond of music, and as my family were musical in their tastes, we used to perform various glees and choruses, in which Mr. Irving took a lively interest.

————————

Jaffray goes on to tell of what might have turned into an unpleasant incident between neighbors. A brook ran through the Jaffray property and on through Sunnyside to the river. Irving had diverted some of its water for his duck pond, his beautiful "Little Mediterranean," and kept a proud eye on his inland sea. As he wrote a friend, "I remained from church today to mend my dam and other profane occupations."

Jaffray decided to use the brook as a water supply for his own estate. He tried to dam it and control it, but the brook was stubborn. He might have persevered but with precise timing Irving sent a poem, dedicated to Jaffray's little daughter, Florence, that ended with the lines:

Irving's last dinner away from home was at Willow Brook, estate of his friend and neighbor, Edward S. Jaffray. Irving's half-emptied wine glass was carefully preserved

But soon it appeared that this brave little brook
    Defied the Laird of Jaffray's skill,
For though he dammed the little brook, and rammed the little brook,
    The little brook still ran down hill.

Then the Sunnyside ducks again plucked up heart
    And got over their quanda-ry,
And the little brook still runs on to Sunnyside pond
    And the mighty Tappan Sea.

"This brave little brook . . ."

10:30 down train in order to keep a very important engagement in town. When I reached the railway track I found that the only possible way of proceeding any further was by wading through water up to my knees! So I had to go back and lose my train. This seems to me an outrage. I have no horses and my only way of getting about is by train. Your Board has allowed Mr. Irving to close a right-of-way on which I have travelled for over 40 years without first insisting that the new road be properly finished. Will you please bring to the notice of your Board the above facts and have a remedy applied.

Very truly yours,

HOWARD S. JAFFRAY

Jaffray's apology came in the form of three lines in a poem ostensibly written by Florence, with a nod to Hiawatha:

How my Papa, very selfish,
Tried to dam up all the water,
Tried to keep more than he ought to. . . .

Heavier hands might have made a contribution to the law of water rights.

Forty years later another Mr. Irving and another Mr. Jaffray did not handle things so well, as the following letter attests:

New York, Oct. 26th, 1897

H. H. Cannon, Esq.
Dear Sir

This morning I went down the new road made by Mr. Irving, meaning to catch the

One of Washington Irving's friends in particular stands out in the very fact that he was not a businessman. John McVickar was a college professor, writer, and Episcopal clergyman. Early in the 1850's he bought the property immediately to the south of Irving on the other side of Sunnyside Lane. A widower, trying to care for four young orphaned grandchildren, he found at Dearman-Irvington pre-

The Reverend John McVickar whose genial, learned company Irving enjoyed

45

cisely the situation he needed.

The Professor and Irving became close friends. They lived within hailing distance of each other, they shared the procession of literary giants that came to each of them— William Cullen Bryant, Oliver Wendell Holmes, Thackeray. The Professor welcomed the sight of his friend briskly mounting the path from Sunnyside in his "oldfashioned black summer dress, with 'pumps' and white stockings, and broad Panama hat and the sound of his throaty greeting as he took his accustomed seat on the veranda." They rocked and talked and enjoyed the sweep of the river. They saw that neither's trees interfered with the other's view, and together did battle against the common enemy, the railroad.

As the 1850's came to a close Irving's health was failing. When he died November 29, 1859, his friend George Morgan wrote:

At about 9 o'clock in the evening I was suddenly called to Sunnyside by the announcement of his gardener that Mr. Irving was very ill. I instantly hurried there. We found him on the floor of his bedroom, surrounded by his two nieces and his nephew, Mr. Pierre M. Irving, with whom he had passed the evening in his usual health and spirits. His life was extinct. Very soon all the members of the family left, bowed in the deepest grief. My gardener, that night, prepared his body for the grave, and I, alone in his parlor, wrote to Mr. Bryant of the *Evening Post,* of the circumstances of his departure and of the great loss the whole world had sustained.

Edward Jaffray spoke for his friends:

The death of Mr. Irving was an irreparable loss to the neighborhood where he had lived so long. It seemed to create a great blank—which still continues, though he has been gone so many years.

Civil War — The home front

[WEL]

On a map of the Town of Greenburgh dated 1857, there is an insert of the village of Irvington. A hotel and six stores, a shoe shop, real estate office, and a blacksmith shop existed then. There were twenty-seven dwellings along the Main avenue and the side streets. In addition, the map indicates eleven homes and a blacksmith shop in Abbotsford and twenty-six homes along the turnpike, plus the rectory, the manse, two churches, the public school, and a private school in a building at 111 North Broadway. In 1855 the old one-room school house had been abandoned and replaced by a new one-story brick school house nearer the center of the village.

The population of Irvington in 1860, according to its first independent census, was 599. But in 1860 no one knew if there would ever be another census in the United States.

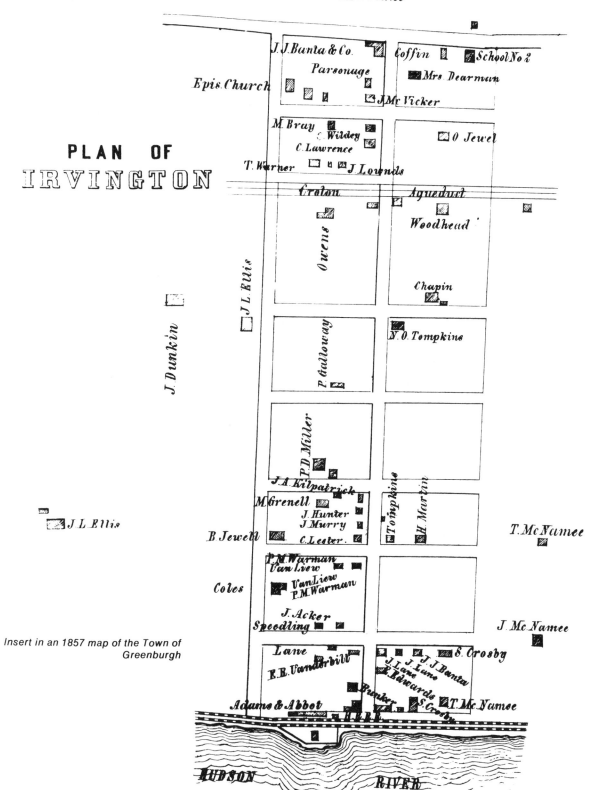

PLAN OF
IRVINGTON

Presb Ch

E. Blunt

J. J. Banta & Co.

Coffin   School No 2

Parsonage

Mrs. Dearman

Epis. Church

J. McVicker

M. Bray

C. Wildey

O. Jewel

C. Lawrence

T. Warner   J. Lownds

Croton   Aqueduct

Woodhead

Owens

Chapin

J. L. Ellis

N. O. Tompkins

J. Dunkin

P. Galloway

P. D. Miller

J. A. Kilpatrick

M. Grenell

J. Hunter

J. Murry

Tompkins

H. Martin

T. McNamee

J. L. Ellis

B. Jewell

C. Lester.

P. M. Warman

Van Liew

Coles

Van Liew
P. M. Warman

J. Acker

Speedling

J. McNamee

Lane   S. Crosby

J. J. Banta

E. E. Vanderbilt

J. Lane
E. Edwards

S. Crosby   T. McNamee

Adams & Abbot   Bunker

Insert in an 1857 map of the Town of
Greenburgh

HUDSON   RIVER

Soon after Lincoln's election South Carolina seceded. Civil war loomed.

It was clear that maintenance of the federal forts in Charleston harbor—Moultrie and Sumter—weakly garrisoned by two under-staffed companies—would be critical. Should the forts be reinforced?

To Irvington's James Hamilton it was a time to act. He needed New York militiamen and he needed money for what he proposed —nothing less than a privately backed relief expedition to the forts. To finance it he turned to two of his Irvington neighbors. Here is his brief account:

The next day, Saturday, December 29, 1860 I went to New York where I found the General at his office and talked the project over with him. He fully approved what I proposed and engaged to give me four hundred men, as good artillerists as could be wished. Having that assurance, I went to Wall Street to make arrangements; saw Moses H. Grinnell who said at once, "Go on—you shall have as much money as you want." I told him that I could contribute one-third, he one-third and Mr. John E. Williams another third.

The offer went to the President, but it was refused. Three and one half months later a telegraph key clattered in a downtown Montgomery, Alabama, office, and the order went

Detail of map, 1857, showing the newly named Irvington

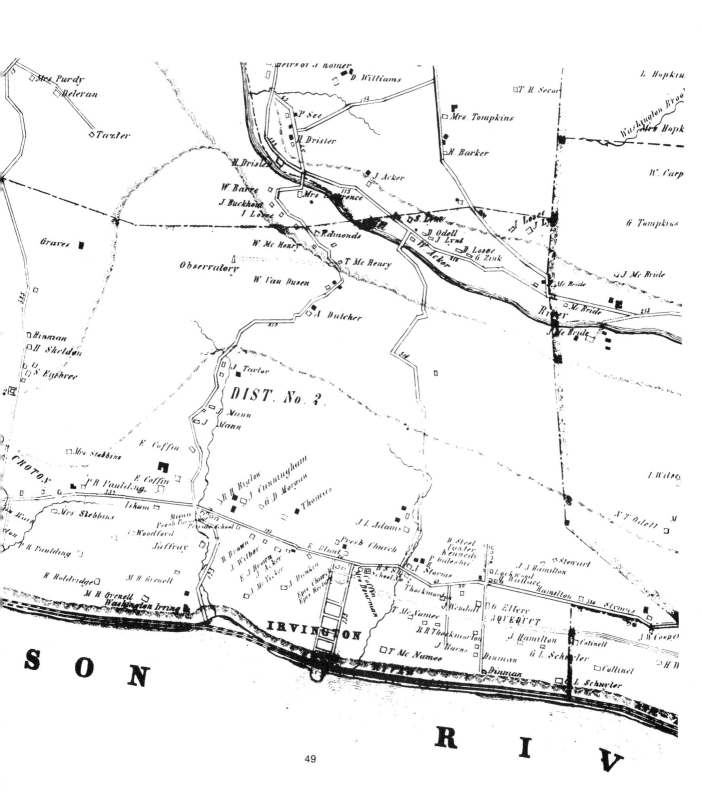

Mrs Purdy

Deleran

Taxter

heirs of J Homer

D Williams

T H Secor

L Hopkin

P See

Mrs Tompkins

Washington Broo

Mrs Hopk

H Drister

H Barker

W Carp

H Drister

W Barne

J Acker

J Buckhout

Mrs Lawrence

I Losee

S Lyne

J Losee

J L

G Tompkins

Graves

J Edmonds

D Odell

J Lynt

J Losee

W McHenry

W Acker

G Zink

Observatory

T McHenry

J McBride

J McBride

W Van Dusen

McBride

A Dutcher

River

McBride

McBride

J Taylor

DIST. No. 2

J Mann

J Mann

Mrs Stebbins

E Coffin

J Wilse

CROTON

E Coffin

R H Biglow

J Cunningham

N T Odell

M

P R Paulding

G D Moran

Thomas

Isham

Mann

Mrs Stebbins

J L Adams

H Steel

Taxter

Kennedy

P Gileshire

Stewart

J A Hamilton

Woodford

Presb Pars

Public School

B Brown

Jaffray

J Wilber

E Blunt

Presb Church

Jack Wogel

Wallace

Hamilton

Strnes

H Holdridge

M H Grenell

E J Brown

J McVicker

J Dunkin

R N SC

School No

Storms

J W

Wendall

M H Grenell

Washington Irving

J McAcker

Epis Church
Epis Rectory

Coffin
See Beaman

Thockmort

G Ellery

AQUEDUCT

SON

IRVINGTON

T McNamee

H R Thockmorton

J Burns

Drman

J Hamilton

Collinet

J W Cooper

RIV

T McNamee

Dinman

G L Schuyler

Collinet

H W

J Schuyler

49

John H. McCullagh, whose Irvington home is shown below, was one of New York City's famous police captains. He joined the force at the time of the draft riots

over the wires that sent the first shell bursting over Sumter.

The Civil War had begun.

Irvington sent its quota of men to battle, but only once during the war did direct violence brush Irvington. Congress had enacted a draft law in 1863, which by any modern standards would be considered a monstrosity. The first drawings took place in New York City on Saturday, July 11, 1863, and full scale rioting flared against the draft. A Negro orphanage was burned. Violence spread across the city in a wave of looting and burning.

The Westchester draft rolls were a target, but there was time to set up a defense. Special police were brought into Irvington and quartered in the old red schoolhouse building at Sunnyside Lane. James Hamilton was well into his seventies, but he accepted the challenge to take a command position. The following extracts from his letters reflect something of the fear that swept the area:

In my letter yesterday, I informed you of the measures taken to resist the mob in our neighborhood and Tarrytown. At present all is quiet, with threatenings, however, at all the landing places along the river. There is a large foreign population in Yonkers, in the pistol factory and other manufactories, who will be compelled to yield to the rioters and maybe brought into the field against us . . .

A body of rioters went on their way, from the south part of the town of Greenburg, advancing to Tarrytown, with music and flags. They endeavored by threats to compel men in the fields to stop work and go along

The name of Washington Irving dominated the area, even to the Civil War Camp Irving in Tarrytown

with them. When in their course they learned from our scouts that we were prepared for them, they stopped at the roadside and scattered.

Federal troops were detached and brought to New York from General Meade's victorious army at Gettysburg. The city was calmed, and order was restored.

51

Old time Sunday

WHEN PROFESSOR MC VICKAR came to Irvington he had had other plans besides establishing a home. He had hoped to found a school and then a college, "St. Barnabas." With stone taken from a quarry on the site of the present Rutter house he built what is now the rectory of St. Barnabas and the first section of the present church as a school and a chapel. At the dedication in 1853 he is reported to "have alluded with deep feeling to the joy of hearing for the first time since creation the rocks and the hills around re-echoing to the sound of the church-going bell."

The project was short-lived. The chapel went on to be the present Episcopal Church of St. Barnabas.

In 1853 a vigorous group founded the Irvington Presbyterian Church. The initial vote was taken in June, the cornerstone laid in August, and the church dedicated barely three months later on November 12th. In

St. Barnabas' Church and Rectory grew from this original Chapel School and Parsonage

time the Presbyterians built a new church across Broadway and the Roman Catholic Church of the Immaculate Conception took over the former property.

Churches meant Sundays and Jennie Black offers her childhood memory of Sundays in Irvington:

The Good Book says that God created Heaven and Earth in six days and rested the seventh day. To me it was ever a source of wonder, in view of the above, why everyone in our household worked harder on Sunday than on any other day of the week.

When I was a child, Sunday was almost a nightmare to me. My dear father and mother, both being of pious nature, took it for granted that we children should be likewise. I was obliged to rise at an earlier hour and breakfast at eight o'clock. This was followed by family prayers at nine, and then off to Sunday School and Church. We always walked. Father said the coachman should have the day with his family.

The procession started, father wearing his Sunday high silk hat and long black coat, with mother on his arm in her best bonnet, camel's hair shawl, and black lace mitts. In summer, the shawl was of black Chantilly lace and she carried a funny little parasol made of the same lace, lined with white silk, and with a hinged stick which could be bent at any angle. It amused me greatly. I held father's other hand, all dressed up in my silk frock with high neck and long sleeves (every week-day in summer I wore low neck and short sleeves and was happy), new shoes and hat, and—most uncomforta-

Miss Daisy Rutter, at the age of 8, dressed
for an old time Irvington Sunday

The Church built in three months by the Presbyterians became
the Roman Catholic Church of the Immaculate Conception, which
was destroyed by fire

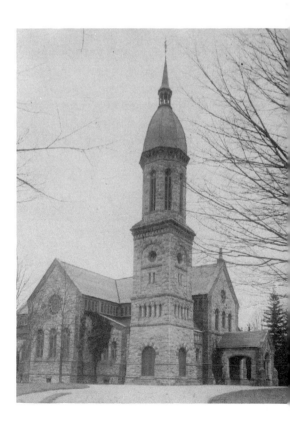

The old Methodist Church, destroyed by fire in 1908, present site of
the Isabel K. Benjamin Community Center

The "new" Presbyterian Church designed by James Renwick, Jr.
architect of New York's Grace Church and St. Patrick's Cathedral.
The Tiffany glass windows were designed by the famous Louis
Comfort Tiffany of Irvington

ble of all—kid gloves! Even when we lived on the high hill at the Bierstadt house, rain or shine, we walked. And oh, such a high hill, and such heat in summer!

In those days father was the Sunday School superintendent and mother was the teacher of the Bible class; my sister was also a teacher, beside being a member of the choir. I, at the age of four, was placed in the infant class. Later I went to church with my mother, where I sat in our family pew and listened to a long tedious discourse, of which I understood nothing.

Do you wonder that I sometimes begged to go into the choir loft, where my father and sister sang in the voluntary choir?

In those days we had what was called a water organ, pumped by hand. One could see the water rise and fall in the indicator as the pressure rose and fell. The first morning I went, the sight intrigued me the moment my eyes fell upon the water tank and the small boy who did the pumping by the side of the console. Being a musical child I determined to induce that boy (like Tom Sawyer and the painting of his famous fence) to let me pump the organ. Suddenly a bright idea! I had a penny in my glove left over from the five pennies my mother had given me for the Sunday School missionary box and which I had secreted, hoping to buy a pickle for myself down at the corner grocery store the following day. I would offer this to my new-found organ-pumping friend. He succumbed at the first glance and handed me the much desired handle.

This was my first office in the Presbyterian Church where I have since played the organ, sung in the choir, taught Sunday School, and worshipped for sixty-five years. But nothing has ever given me the thrill I received as a small child when I realized that *I* was making the organ GO.

The above happened many years ago. Since that time the interior of our lovely ivy-covered grey-stone Presbyterian Church has been redecorated by Louis Tiffany, once a member of the church, the old glass windows replaced by his choice Tiffany glass with an especial design for each window.

The village comes of age

In 1872 IRVINGTON WAS INCORPORATED as a village—but not soon enough to prevent its northern section being included in the Village of Tarrytown, incorporated two years earlier.

It had been an unhappy loss, and years later Jennie Black recorded the old resentment:

Just how the change in our northern boundary occurred, I could never find out to my full satisfaction. Some say this calamity happened over night, so to speak, when our officials were napping or away on a va-

The River Villages, circa 1867

cation. But this I know, that fully a dozen of our most prominent citizens and their magnificent estates were suddenly taken from Irvington territory and the village boundary line was moved to the center of Sunnyside Lane. . . . Even today many of the present owners of these old estates use "Irvington-on-Hudson" on their letter heads and receive their mail through the Irvington post office.

. . . The part that most saddened our hearts was the fact that Irving's home, "Sunnyside," for whom Irvington was named, no

Lyndhurst, one of the mansions "kidnapped" by Tarrytown

longer rests in the town in which he originally thought he lived.

Despite the loss to Tarrytown, Irvington prospered. Its churches were established, its local merchants and places of entertainment were thriving, and there was a local industry, Lord and Burnham, which within five years gained a reputation in the greenhouse field from coast to coast. New and articulate people were playing variations on the village theme.

hats may have swirled over the frozen ponds, the ladies may have taken their afternoon drives from the big houses, but it was not quite all Currier and Ives. Like any home-made quilt Irvington was made of many patches.

The first Board of Trustees stepped up briskly to the immediate demands of the new village. To meet police and "extraordinary" expenses for the first year they imposed a special tax of $1000.

Firefighting was still a neighborhood function with bucket brigades using any available water. It was a long jump to the first functioning department, organized in 1880 with 37 volunteers. Three years later the Village water system was installed and firefighters

Growing pains

THE NEED TO BECOME A VILLAGE, in control of its own destiny, was not academic. Problems were pressing in. The water supply was inadequate. The unpaved streets were often either mired in mud or beds of dust. At the whim of bank-side owners the brooks running down to the Hudson could be open sewers. Garbage was often informally recycled by stray pigs and goats. The flashing skates and the wide skirts and the Empress Eugenie

Fire alarms were sounded by striking this iron ring

had something to work with. Probably there was no finer moment than in 1911 when Irvington said goodbye to the fire horses and welcomed a bright red new combination chemical and hose Locomobile.

An early order of business for the new Board was to impose a rational order of things. They passed eleven ordinances:

1. Intoxicated persons; disturbing the peace.
2. Closing times of establishments selling intoxicating beverages.
3. Littering the village streets.
4. Removing rock or paving from the streets.

The first Firehouse was on North Ferris Street

Durable beauties: two White fire engines of the early 1920's
Below, the 1888 Hose Jumper Contest team

5. Safety of persons walking on the streets.

6. Removal of dead animals.

7. Performing or entertaining without permit.

8. Bathing without proper attire.

9. Police regulations and arrests.

10. Obstructing policeman in performance of his duties.

11. Damaging property.

Not only dead animals but live ones on the loose in the village were creating problems. The trustees met to hear complaints, and they heard them—about wandering cows, horses, mules, sheep, goats, pigs, geese, and dogs. Ordinances were passed to control the animal nuisance, but for many years the village pound was an important adjunct of law and order.

Enforcement of these ordinances and police protection was provided by a single constable, Peter M. Warman, appointed by the Board at an annual salary of $500. In July 1872 the constable reported to Mr. F. A. Foster, President of the Board of Trustees:

In passing through D Street South you will find several pest holes in a very malarious condition for want of proper drainage. Also F Street is in a very filthy condition at its southern extremity, by depositing coal ashes, garbage, soap suds, and fish water endangering the health of the village to a very great degree.

In D Street North near R. Abercrombie's stable stands a box on the sidewalk for depositing manure in, and very offensive to the tenants adjacent.

In the rear of F. Timms is a place where garbage, offal, and dirty water is thrown creating an intolerable stench to the surrounding premises, likely to produce disease and death.

The above being all respectfully submitted

I remain your most obt. svt.

P. M. WARMAN P. C.

A policeman's lot is not a happy one

IRVINGTON OF THE 1870's AND 1880's was lively. The kettle periodically blew off steam. Often the edge between control and exuberance was Irvington's police.

In 1875, the Trustees spelled out their lone constable's duties:

. . . That there may be a clear understanding. . . . It being your business to preserve order and to protect persons and property throughout the village, it is required of you that you be at or near the Hudson River Depot from 7:30 a.m. to 9 a.m. and 5 p.m.

A thriving village, 1870. The merchants of Irvington were:

Adams, C. A. & Bro—Grocers, A Street

Anderson, James—Plumbing, Gas Fitting and Dealer in Hardware, A Street

Calder, Alex—Builder, Saw and Moulding Mill, opposite Depot

Cannon, H. H.—Grain, Flour, Feed, Etc., A Street

Drinkle, John—Grocer, corner Main Street and Post Road

Evans, H.—Propr. of Irvington Hotel, opposite Depot

Lawrence, C. W.—Carpenter and Builder, Main Street

Mason, John—Express, Main Street

Peck, G. W.—House and Sign Painter, Main Street

Storms and Lockwood—Coal, Wood and Building Materials, opposite Depot

Walker, Wm.—Carpenter and Builder, D Street

Wilder, C. S.—Wheelwright and Blacksmithing, F Street

59

to 6 p.m., and that, at least once daily, you traverse Broadway from Sunny Side Lane to the South line of the village. Besides this you will be expected to respond to the requests of any of the inhabitants for protection against molestation or trespass, as far as in your judgement the law may authorize and the circumstances may require you to do so.

The Constable was also to keep a watchful eye against unlawful handling of rubbish and manure, waterway stoppages, and the condition of the streets. He was to be alert if vagrants or tramps were passing through the village and was to protect the residents from annoyance and depredation. The instructions continued:

As regards your duties as lamplighter, you are instructed to keep lamps in perfect order, filled and cleaned, to light them at a suitable hour, and not to commence extinguishing the lights before 11 o'clock.

Not only were the hours marathon, but the Constable was admonished:

In all your dealings with the inhabitants of the village, or with strangers, you are expected to be courteous and patient, executing your duties firmly, but striving to be as little offensive to the Community as may be consistent with a strict and full execution of its provisions.

The Constable takes a brief pause in front of the Tiffany house

From the very outset the Constable's pursuit of duty had its drama. Officer Warman, in the same letter in which he gave such a doleful report of the village streets, advised the Village President of occurrences at John Byrnes', on West Clinton Avenue.

In compliance with your order of the 18th inst, I called on Mr. John Burns [Byrnes], informing him of a complaint having been made to your Board against him for keeping a disorderly house, and being a resort for disorderly persons, etc, etc. To which he pleads justification, on the following grounds, to wit, that he having purchased said premises anterior to any of the present population becoming residents, that since their occupancy of the surrounding lands they have hemmed in his premises with high fences, trees and shrubbery to such an extent as to make his grounds almost valueless, that he had made strenuous efforts to sell out his place to them, they not being willing to purchase the same, he takes this method to retrieve his losses, arguing as a citizen having the right to carry on dancing and merrymaking with his family, or any other persons who may feel disposed, to visit him for such purposes, and either to give away or sell his Lager saying that he will test his right so to do to the full extent of the Law, yielding only by compulsion of Law.

Sunday 21st he kept the place open, numerous persons, male, female, and children on platform, closing the place on my approach. Passing down below Mr. Carey's residence and returning; place open again and numbers of new recruits collecting. All other places within the corporation closed in front, with a slight back door traffic.

It turned out that John Byrnes was not so much opposing the angels as delivering a commercial message. Years later Charles F. Huston, then in his 70's and a life-long resident of East Clinton Avenue, told a reporter from the Yonkers *Herald Statesman* what had happened. The July 12, 1934 issue of the paper carried the story in a write-up of the Abbotsford section of the village.

. . . There was a junk-man in Abbotsford, famous throughout the county under the title of "Cheap Johnny Byrnes." An enterprising person, he used to exchange dress goods or cash for old scrap iron, brass and the like. At one time, however, he wanted to sell his property and couldn't get a buyer. He decided to make a nuisance of his place.

He hung out a large sign—"Cheap Johnny Byrnes: I buy and sell fat, rags, bottles and junk"—where all the ladies and gentlemen of the neighborhood could see it. But that wasn't all. He built a dance platform and a rough clap-board saloon in his junk yard, and advertised Saturday night dances. Music was furnished by a bagpiper, Patsy Kerrigan; a violinist, James Gorey; and a cornet player, according to Mr. Huston. The place attracted a host of patrons, largely workers in the carpet factory in Yonkers. These men would come to the Saturday night dances, hitch their rigs to the neighbors' fences, and carouse till late Sunday morning.

Meanwhile their horses would eat the neighbors' shrubbery and kick in the pickets of the fences. This was too much for the good people of Clinton Avenue to stand, and David Dows finally bought "Cheap Johnny" out.

The Irvington police force was a mere ten years old when the cry of police brutality was raised. In a letter dated October 19, 1882 the

Alex Byrnes, a relative of John Byrnes, in front of the Huston house on East Clinton Avenue, which had been purchased with a $5 deposit

respected Eliphalet Wood complained to the Board of Trustees:

It becomes my unpleasant duty to report to your Board of an unprovoked assault made upon my person by policeman Wm O'Brien. It occurred this morning between the hours of ten and eleven o'clock directly in front of Wm Fariel's market.

His language at first was abusive and violent. I made an effort to evade an encounter, and quietly get out of his way, but in vain. He followed me and seized me by the collar repeatedly, and made threats on my life.

Yours respectfully,
ELIPHALET WOOD

What triggered Policeman O'Brien's considerable temper and what came of the incident is lost in the mists.

The pencilled draft of a letter from the Village Clerk to Policeman Henry Raisch in 1898 indicates that the Trustees of the day were finding it necessary to watch the watchman:

At a regular meeting held June 7, 1898 the Clerk was instructed to inform you that complaints had been entered against you relating to the careless way in which you attend to your duties as policeman, and am further instructed to say that a change must be made for the benefit of the public, and the Board desires that you keep out of all saloons in this village while in uniform or on duty, and in case of absence from the village a permit must be granted to you by the President.

"A fruitful source of disease"

ANOTHER OF THE TRUSTEES' early actions was to appoint a Board of Health and a Health Officer. They were almost immediately confronted by an outbreak of small-pox that threatened to become an epidemic. Moving promptly they imposed effective quarantine measures and vaccinated more than 600 residents.

The streets on either side of Main Street had originally been privately owned by adjacent landowners. One resident had even maintained his own private fence across Dutcher Street at the south line of his property to keep out wandering animals and, as he put it, "other encroachments."

To deal with conditions that were threatening to create a serious health hazard the Trustees appointed a Street Committee. In March 1875, a year after they took office, the Street Committee reported:

When they entered upon the discharge of their duties, the committee found that the time had come when it was necessary to devise some system of grading and drainage

62

Board sidewalk on muddy Main Street

both to prevent damage to property and to subserve the sanitary interest of the inhabitants, at least in the thickly settled portion of the village.

They found that from Broadway to the river the surface water, with few exceptions, flowed over the streets and private property, that grading of many of the streets was such that water collected in gutters and pools; that many cellars and sunken lots were, during most of the year, filled with stagnant water, a fruitful source of disease and epidemic.

The committee therefore adopted a plan designed to remedy these evils. They determined to change the grade of the side streets so that each street should deliver the water which might fall upon it, and the

property adjoining, into the channels provided to carry it away.

This work has been satisfactorily completed from Broadway as far west as "B" Street. The remainder can be easily completed at a moderate expense during the coming summer.

. . . sunken lots and wet cellars are dry already, and it is believed a beneficial effect on the health of the village is noticeable . . .

———

At one point the Committee notes that work had been suspended "for lack of funds." But improvements continued. Streets were repaired, Broadway was graveled from the Tarrytown to the Dobbs Ferry line; it was proposed to grade and gravel Harriman Road.

By 1875 the village was on a sound footing. The way would not be all smooth—a point that could not be better made than in letters from the files of the Board of Trustees.

Drainage, for example, may have been solved, but sidewalks were a different matter. In 1879, the Board required owners on both sides of Main Street and on the west side of Broadway from Tarrytown to Dobbs Ferry to put in bluestone flagging sidewalks four feet wide. A storm broke over the Trustees. Landowners who would bear the cost raised a hue and cry, and petitions poured in:

. . . Defer the work until the return to more prosperous times or . . . provide that the said sidewalks shall be made of gravel, to be in keeping with the roadbed of the streets.

Our village is justly considered the most beautiful and attractive in America, and unsurpassed in the world. A stone pavement may be desireable and appropriate for a City, but never for a Park village like Irvington. A gravel walk is more agreeable to walk upon, cheaper and cooler in the summer . . .

If some petitioners considered Irvington unsurpassed in the world, others protested:

. . . that the flag sidewalks would distract from the rural character of the village. And real estate in the neighborhood can hardly be sold or rented due to the fact that the pestilential character of the village having been so lately been noised abroad and even

ILLAGE OF

NGTON

0 feet per inch.

881

Charles Harriman

C.S. Frankley

E.C. Gregory

Jas. A. Hamilton Est.

H. H. Cannon

Cyrus W. Field

D. A. Lindley

Edw. Field

WAY

PRIVATE

J. D. Dibble

NEARWOOD

Cyrus W. Field

Whitehouse

F. W. Guiteau

IRVING CLIFF Fairholt WOOD

Mrs. Clarton

Caroline Scott 12 a.

William H. Smith 12 a.

Harriman

Col. Chamberlain

Miss R. Wendell

Jas. Cannon

Fletcher Harper Est.

Jewell Est.

Lord & Burnham

Mrs. Mellons & Miss Crosby

B. E. Gurnee

J. L. Barney

Greenkill

GLENARM

Ho. Wm. F. Drake

Miss R. Wendel

AVE.

Alexander Hamilton

ST. BARNABAS CH.

CROTON

LODGE & STABLE

S. S. Rubra "EL RETIRO"

D. N. Lorcar

Wm. H. Preston

AQUEDUCT

Geo. W. Smith

"NEVIS"

WELL

TOWER

Mrs. A. J. Orton

J. F. Adams

D. C. Hoy's

UNION SCHOOL

A. L. Barney

CALV. CH.

M. E.

F. Kinport

John Casey

Jos. Steiner

W. F. Cary Jr.

CLINTON

Dunham Est.

D. N. Barney Est.

GRAPERY

John D. Hair's "LYNWOOD"

CHARLTON HALL

David Dows

F. A. Foster

GREEN HO.

Philip Schuyler

W. Walker

A. B. Barney

Mary A. Vaga 9 a.

STATION A

Charles Harriman LUMBER & COAL YD PLAN. MILL

STON RIVER

been commented upon by the English press.

———————

The President of the village left to spend the summer in Europe, and on his return the Board bowed to the opposition. Paved sidewalks would await a more propitious time.

The gaslight era

OVER THE YEARS the Trustees obviously did some protesting of their own. A forbear of

the Consolidated Edison Company replied:

GLOBE GAS LIGHT COMPANY, LIMITED
115 Broadway, New York

New York, May 3rd, 1888

Mr. T. W. Crisfield, Village Clerk
Irvington-on-Hudson, New York

Dear Sir:
Your favor of May 2nd is received with our lighting bill of April 30th, (21 nts ltg in April, amount, $62.06/100), returned for correction in the number of nights charged for.

In reply thereto, would say that the above bill, we believe to be correct and same was figured in accordance with the monthly report and statement of our superintendent there, Mr. Thos. H. Mann, who reported having lit the lamps on the nights of Apr. 1st to 18th, incl., (18 nts), and Apr. 28 to 30th., (3 nts). A total of 21 nights.

Our Mr. Kroberger informed us that he had explained to you, (when on a visit of inspection there recently), how it would occur at times this year that there would be more than 20 nights lighted in some months. This is owing to the circuits of the moon this year, by which it will frequently occur that there are two periods of darkness in a month.

Now, we would call your attention to the marked clauses in the enclosed blank form of contract . . . by which it is provided that where the number of nights to be lit each month is less than the whole number, such number of nights lighted shall take place on nights between the moons and shall be known as lunar months.

Therefore, as there are more lunar than calendar months in the year, it will of necessity occur at times that there will be more than 20 nights lighted each calendar month.

You will see, therefore, that the service has been consistently performed, and that there is not an over-charge in the number of nights on the April bill.

However, if your Board of Trustees desire that the lamps be lighted only 20 nights each calendar month, we certainly have no objections thereto, since there will be less material used and less labor to pay for each month.

Please to advise us at your earliest convenience of the wishes of the Board in this matter, so that we may issue instructions at once if only 20 nts are to be lighted in each calendar month. We would suggest, however, that your Village would be better lighted by adhering to the lunar system.

Trusting that the above explanation is understood by you, and that our bill, (for service performed), will be audited. We remain,

Yours respectfully,

N.Y. & N.J. Globe Gas Light Co., Limited
F. A. SEAMAN, JR. SECY.

Enclosed we beg leave to return the April bill.

Winter Harvest—ice cutting on Halsey's Pond

The Village Pump House sat over the original water supply, a 600-foot deep well

Water, water!

[WEL]

When the village was incorporated it lacked a proper water supply. The large estates depended on private reservoirs, fed by springs that had a dual purpose in also supplying a quantity of ice for refrigeration. Other homes depended upon wells from which water was pumped by hand to large wooden tanks placed in the attic to increase

This watery chapel housed the outlet pipe which ran from pump house to reservoir

the supply and pressure. Large cisterns received the water from roofs which was used principally for laundry and watering the animals.

In the village proper there were three public wells along Main Street that were maintained by the street commissioner. Several wells and springs augmented the drinking water supply of the residents in the area. Statistics show that there was a gradual increase in so-called "sewer fever and baby colic" as the population increased and a distinct decrease when a proper water and sewer system was installed at a later date.

Eventually, beginning in 1883, Irvington constructed its own water system and supplemented it by withdrawals of water en route to New York City, for many years tapping

into the old aqueduct that runs the length of
the village. But despite all efforts, water remained a problem, and over the years swirls
of protest descended on the Board.

An undated letter about 1910 reads:

My dear Mr. Mayor—
As the mayor I appeal as a *last* resource to
you failing *everywhere else* to find anyone
in the village that assumes *any* responsibility or *knows* anything about anything;
not only has the water been turned off
these last weeks *hours* at a time—but when
it comes on—it is so *filthy* we let it *run
hours* to try to clear it (for which you
charge us on water bill) but now it is completely filthy for over one week—absolutely
"mud" and a vile odor— Health officers
should be called in, really == That I am
billed—with my $3,000.00 walk torn up all
summer—No entrance to get into my home
from Broadway—litter and *filth* at my entrances and fence—life is not *worth paying*
for in money for taxes to be made
miserable—No system—no thought of the
people who PAY for this—just the "privileged Class" of State, County and Village—
to do *as they* please—and have us foot the
bills—which we will soon be *unable* to do;
and then when *we* are bled to death—how
will the "privileged Class" be *paid* for their
incompetency and high handedness—This
and many more things there are to com-
plain of but the *health* menace in the filthy
water, and the entrances from road, and the
property destroyed are the most vital—I
have *tried* everything before bothering you
—but in every case received the answer
"We have nothing to do with *that*."

*Crawford's insurance maps on the following pages
show the village center as of 1889. Details include
residences, businesses, gas and electric facilities,
water mains, hotels, churches, docks, the school,
the depot, saloons, a beer garden and even the
prevailing winds*

69

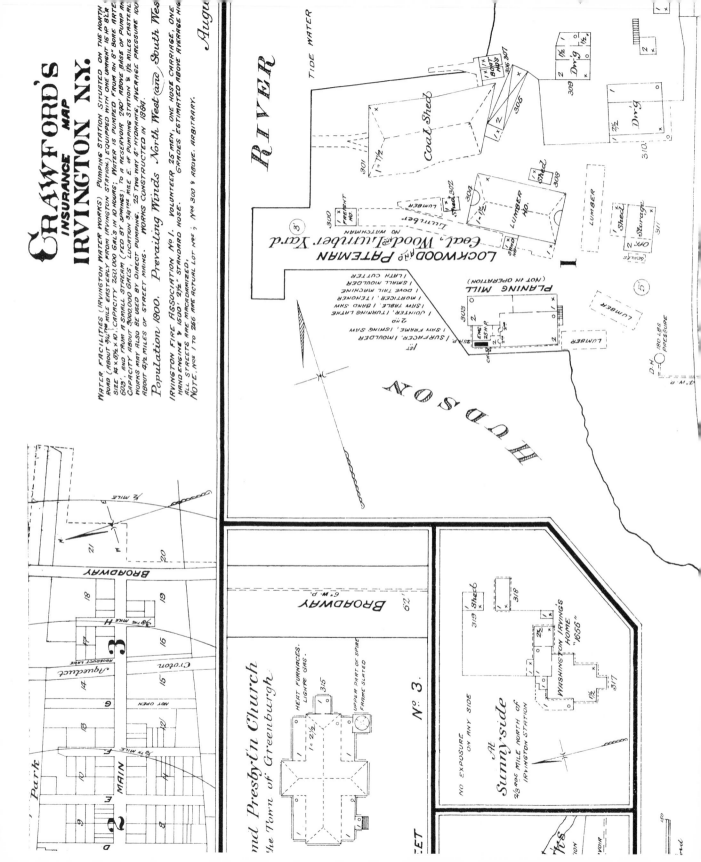

CRAWFORD'S INSURANCE MAP IRVINGTON N.Y.

WATER FACILITIES (IRVINGTON WATER WORKS) PUMPING STATION SITUATED ON THE NORTH ROAD (ABOUT 3/4 THE MILE EASTERLY FROM IRVINGTON STATION.) EQUIPPED WITH ONE UPRIGHT 15 H.P. B'L'R SIZE 14 x 8½ x 10'. CAPACITY 250,000 GALS IN 10 HOURS; WATER IS PUMPED FROM AN 8" BORE ARTE— 603', AND FROM A SMALL STREAM (FED BY SPRINGS); TO A RESERVOIR 240' ABOVE BASE OF PUMP A— CAPACITY ABOUT 300,000 GALS, LOCATION 3/4 THS MILE E. OF PUMPING STATION ¾ ½ MILES EASTER— WORKS MAY ALSO BE USED BY DIRECT PUMPING. 25 TWO WAY 4" HYDRANTS, AVERAGE PRESSURE 100— ABOUT 4½ MILES OF STREET MAINS. WORKS CONSTRUCTED IN 1884.

Population 1800. Prevailing Winds North West and South West

IRVINGTON FIRE ASSOCIATION No. 1. VOLUNTEER 25 MEN, ONE HOSE CARRIAGE, ONE HAND ENGINE & 1500' 2½" STANDARD HOSE. GRADES ESTIMATED ABOVE AVERAGE HIG— ALL STREETS ARE MACADAMIZED.
NOTE: Nos 1 TO 266 ARE ACTUAL LOT Nos ; Nos 300 & ABOVE, ARBITRARY.

RIVER

TIDE WATER

HUDSON

Coal Shed

LOCKWOOD AND PATEMAN
Coal, Wood and Lumber Yard
No WATCHMAN

LUMBER HO.
LUMBER
LUMBER
Storage
Shed
Scales
Off'ce
Sheds

Dry'g
Dry'g

PLANING MILL
(NOT IN OPERATION)

1st | SURFACER, 1 MOULDER
1 SAW FRAME, 1 SWING SAW
2nd
1 JOINTER, 1 TURNING LATHE
1 MORTICER, 1 TENONER
1 DOVE TAIL MACHINE
1 SMALL MOULDER
1 LATH CUTTER

LUMBER
D.H. 180 LBS PRESSURE

BROADWAY
6" W.P.

¼ MILE

21
20
19
18
17
16
15
14
13

3
2

BROADWAY
Aqueduct
Croton
MAIN
Park

NOT OPEN

and Presbyt'n Church
the Town of Greenburgh

HEAT FURNACES.
LIGHTS GAS.

UPPER PART OF SPIRE
FRAME SLATED

No. 3.

No EXPOSURE ON ANY SIDE

At Sunnyside
2/3 RDS MILE NORTH OF
IRVINGTON STATION

WASHINGTON IRVING'S HOME "1656"

Shed
Shed

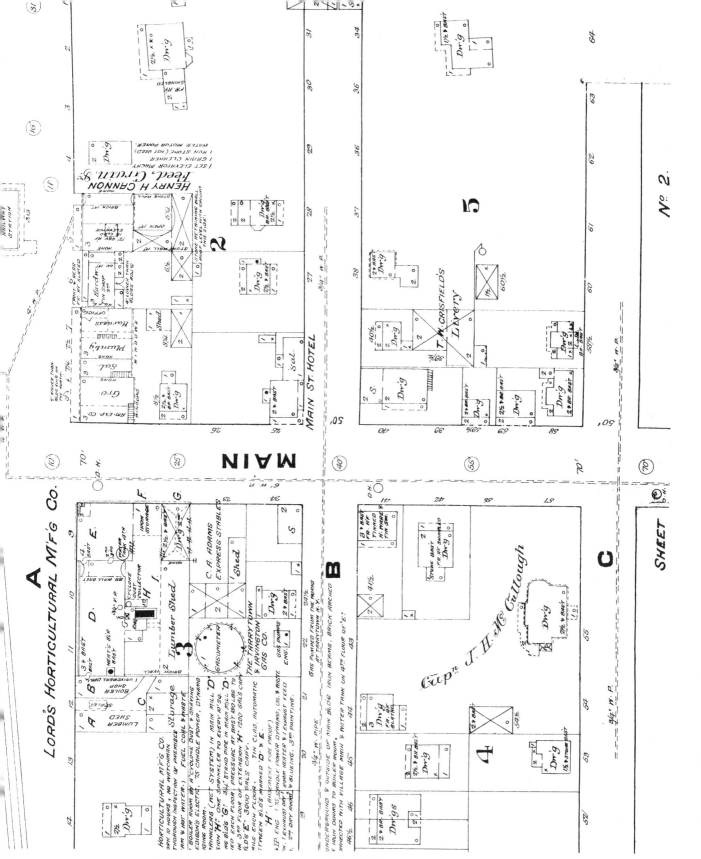

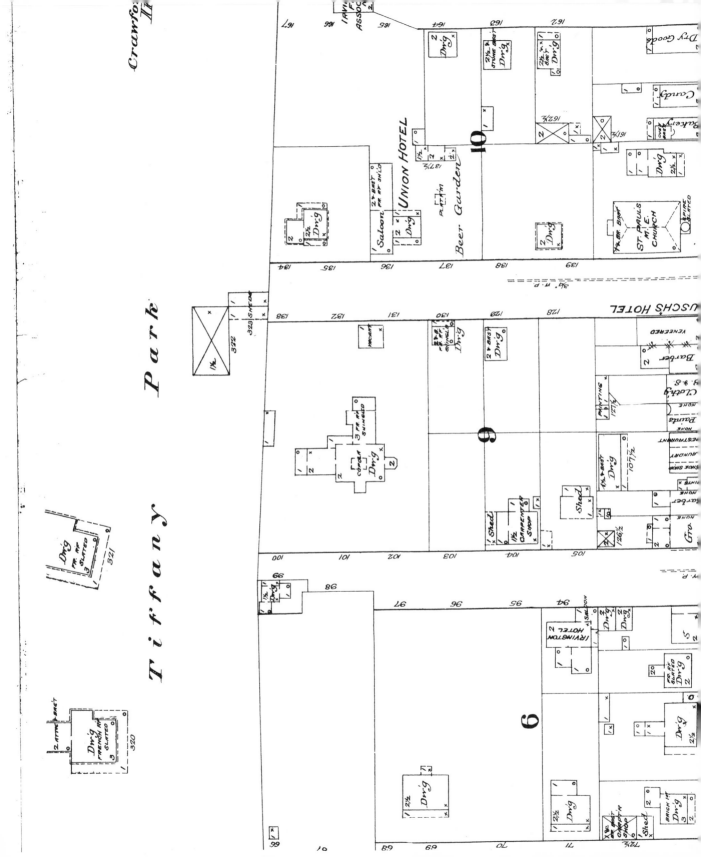

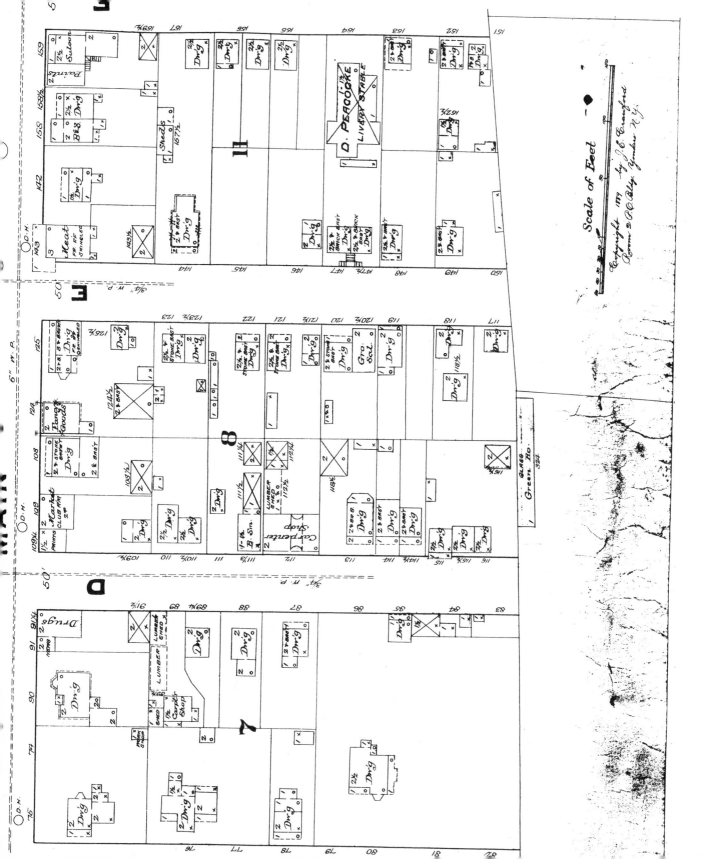

Scale of Feet

Copyright 1889 by J. C. Crawford
Room 2 P. O. Bldg, Yonkers N.Y.

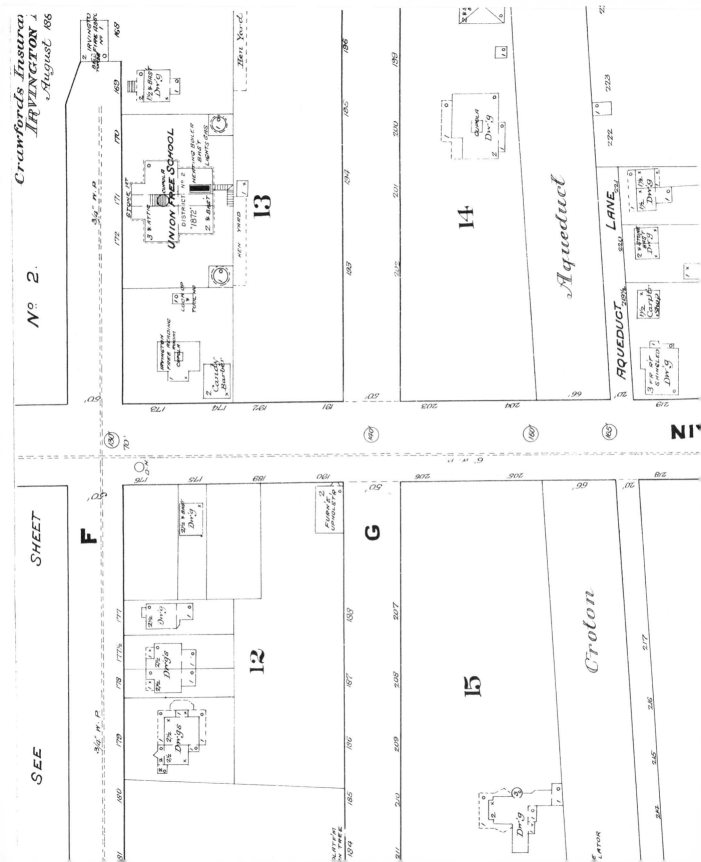

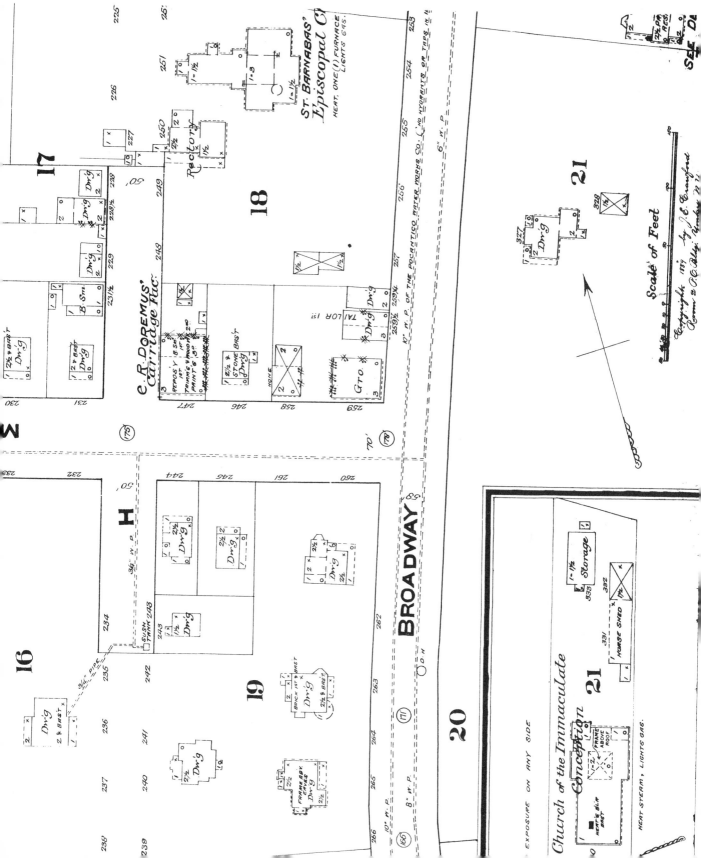

Scale of Feet

Copyright 1889 by J. B. Crawford
From Sanborn & P.O. Bldg, Yonkers N.Y.

17

18

16

H

19

3

20

BROADWAY

ST. BARNABAS'
Episcopal Ch.
HEAT, ONE (1) FURNACE
LIGHTS GAS.

Rectory

e.R. DOREMUS'
Cartridge Mfg.

21

Church of the Immaculate
Conception

21

HEAT, STEAM, LIGHTS GAS.

EXPOSURE ON ANY SIDE

Storage

HORSE SHED

Dw'g

Dw'g

Dw'g

Dw'g

Dw'g

Dw'g

Dw'g

Dw'g

Dw'g

Dw'g

B. Sm.

STONE B'k'st

TAILOR 1st

Gt'o.

Homes, mansions and castles

Aesthetically the village of Irvington offers a spectrum of American architecture. Its houses range in pattern from the simplicity of the pre-Revolutionary salt-box, through the complexities of Hudson River Gothic, Hudson River bracketed, Octagon, mid-19th century Italianate, Greek Revival, split-level ranch, and contemporary glass.

The homes in a community reflect the interests and activity, the aspirations and dreams of the inhabitants . . . [WEL]

The so-called "Half Captain" or story and a half cottage was the most popular during the early portion of the last century. By utilizing the grade, a large portion of the foundation was laid above ground where full sized windows and a door admitted light and air to a combination kitchen and dining room. The unexposed part of the cellar was entered through the kitchen and utilized as storage space for foodstuffs and fuel for the kitchen range and base heaters on the upper floors.

During the latter half of the century the mansard roofed homes appeared and were followed shortly after by the Victorian with its gable roof, bay windows and gingerbread ornamentation.

Many of the large Gothic type homes along

A substantial residence, with gingerbread trim, on Main Street—now the headquarters of Sleepy Hollow Restorations

The home of village father, Justus Dearman

Some village homes were traditional in design. The Morris house on "F" Street was built shortly after 1850 yet reflects 18th century style

A classical mansard-roofed house that stands beside the aqueduct

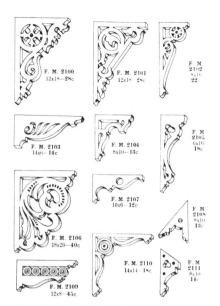

Scroll work brackets from the Foster-Munger Company catalogue

The lumber yard on "B" Street, once the Storm house. Watercolor by Laurence Lustig, 1949

A "Half Captain" Hudson River bracketed cottage

Washington Irving bought his boots and shirts from cobbler Forkhill and his seamstress daughter, Rachel, who lived in this house. Each finely stitched shirt cost 25 cents

Home built in the late '70's by Irvington's first industrialists, Messrs. Lord and Burnham

Broadway had the flat hipped roof altered to the mansard, which gave additional living space in a third floor. This was copied to some extent in the village proper.

Once inside a village home a visitor to Irvington would find a familiar interior.

[WEL]

The most important piece of furniture of the most important room in a home in the late nineteenth century was the kitchen stove that occupied a portion of the wall near the chimney with the coal scuttle and wood box. It heated the water to wash the clothes as well as the flatirons to press them. It popped, fried, broiled and boiled everything from corn to peas, steaks, chops and griddle cakes. It heated water for baths, boiled the clothes and in wet weather, dried them. The oven baked bread, cakes

"There came upon our important townspeople a wave of sentimental fervor (like an epidemic of measles), a desire to bestow on their estates, no matter how small, aesthetic names suggested by nature." —Jennie Prince Black. Here is "The Larches" the Adams-Whitehouse home

From Foster-Munger Company in Chicago ("We furnish the plans, you build the house"); the estimated price was $2,800 to $3,200

A rural kitchen, with Dutch tile wallpaper fashionable in the 1890's, as drawn by Perkins Harnly

and roasts, heated bricks to warm cold feet in bed and dried wet feet as well. The space beneath became a brooder for motherless chicks and a nursery for kittens and pups. The wood box always seemed to be empty and the ash pan full.

The kitchen windows were ornamented with favorite potted flowers, a pot of chives, parsley and sweet geranium for flavoring. The light from these windows cast their shadows on the kitchen table where the food was prepared and served; baked goods were mixed, moulded and cooled. Here baby was bathed, changed and clothed. It became a support for the big brass lamp that provided illumination for reading and homework and a proper light for father to shave. In addition it supported the ironing board and was used as a cutting table for gingham and calico, a tea and coffee table where neighbors and close

friends were entertained.

The kitchen sink was little more than a large zinc or copper basin sunk in a long wide board. It supported a pump that raised water from a well or cistern in the backyard. One end of the surface was slotted and served a dual purpose as a drainboard for dishes and place to prepare vegetables as well as a convenient place to cleanse dirty little feet.

A wall to wall cupboard occupied a corner beside the kitchen door. Here supplies of groceries and canned goods were kept and the vegetables on a lower shelf shared a place for pots and pans. The upper shelves held a bread box, cooky jar and the kitchen dishes.

The outside kitchen door led to a back porch or stoop that contained a zinc-lined wooden icebox where perishable food was stored. The supply of ice was furnished by an iceman who was summoned by placing a card marked "Ice" in a window in view of the street. A covered tin pail was left on the porch each night for the milkman to fill from a large can on his wagon. The amount of milk requested was based on tickets showing the amount purchased from him in advance. An old milk bill indicates the price of whole milk in 1889 to be five cents a quart.

The back stoop was a depository for work clothes, kerosene for the lamps and the usual oil lantern to light the way to the backyard. A space on the wall was reserved for the large wooden washtub used for laundry and the Saturday night bath when the kitchen became the bathroom. The tub was placed near the open oven door in the winter . . .

There was a close relationship among neighbors who shared each other's joys and sorrows. The exchange of skills was not uncommon. The skillful cook exchanged products with the seamstress and the carpenter and the mason joined with the painter and plumber in erecting many village homes. The old-fashioned quilting bee

The Ladies' cooking class of 1889—Jennie Black, President. After the principal course, salad, dessert and coffee "we all went home much the worse for wear."

was popular, and the helping hand at canning time when rows of preserves lined the window sills of the kitchen was unforgettable. The long workday and a six day week left little time for relaxation during the summer months. The Independence Day celebration with its speech-making, fireworks and the usual picnic, circus day and a long day at the county fair in the fall were always family days anticipated with pleasure by everyone.

There never was "another side of the tracks" in Irvington. . . . The villagers were a mixture of businessmen, mechanics and laborers composed of descendants of early settlers and former citizens of the British Isles and central Europe. The close relationship between "up the hill and down the hill" has produced, through the years, a citizen somewhat different from the usual.

Irvington had another kind of home—the so-called "estate." These varied in pretension; the amount of land they occupied ranged from as little as one acre to as much as several hundred.

[WEL]

The houses were designed to suit the taste of the owner, the requirements of the family and the amount of entertainment expected. The majority were constructed of native stone and erected by local craftsmen under the supervision of an architect. Many of the families retained city homes as their official residences and occupied their Irvington estates during the late spring, summer and early fall. The produce of the

Receiving guests for afternoon tea at the Kittle house on North Broadway

David Dows' mansion was torn down by its next owner, Adam K. Luke, to spite high taxes. Afterward he regretted destroying his favorite house

At the Peter Moller house, built in 1854, where the high point of the last reception for Washington Irving was ice cream served in the form of his famous works

From the stones of the Cunningham castle, which had burned down the night before it was to be occupied, the Sayles chateau was built

The Wood-Rutter house that commanded the head of Main Street.
In recent years, it became the site of Fieldpoint.

A contemporary photograph of the Wood-Rutter
drawing room

Strawberry Hill's builder, John Thomas, was killed in
1855 when lightning struck the pitchfork he was carrying
back from haying. The interior plan of the enlarged
house shows the main kitchen on the 2nd floor

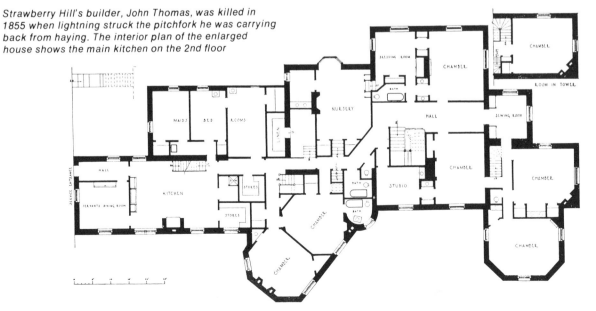

poultry house, dairy and garden were shipped to the city home in special express containers during the winter months . . .

The number of persons employed on an estate was based upon the size of the home and property as well as the requirements of the family. Consider two of the smaller estate owners who jointly protested the destruction of a well used by both families. They claimed, "It is a positive necessity of our families which jointly number some forty persons." The two properties were both under five acres each. The families included the owners, maids, gardeners, and coachmen and their families who lived on the estates. The gardener's cottage or gatehouse, and the coachman's family who lived over or near the coach house all received a portion of the produce from the garden, orchard, poultry house and dairy as perquisites to their salaries. Extra help was hired as the need arose.

The large estate was supervised by a resident superintendent who was qualified to supervise and provide for the care of buildings and grounds and those persons employed. These varied during the seasons and the size of the property. The stable was the responsibility of the coachman who was assisted by one or more grooms.

The spacious lawns were bordered with flowering shrubs and evergreens and closely cropped by staked out sheep or were mowed by the gardener who swung a wide-bladed scythe over its surface.

The sheep and scythe yielded after 1868 to the lawnmower which gradually was improved from a crude reel-type, hand-oper-

The service buildings of Irvington's estates were handsome in their own right.

Above: "Birds Nest" the greystone Victorian Sheeler residence, formerly the gate-house of the Dows-Luke estate
Below: The horses and carriages of Ardsley Towers had luxurious quarters of their own

Even the doves had their gingerbread cotes under the eaves of the Kittle stable

A lacy gazebo on the Beltzhoover swan lake

The Mairs mansion lawns being manicured by one unlucky fellow pushing a lawnmower while his fellow worker cuts in comfort

ated model to a wide-bladed horse mower. Leather boots were attached to the horses' feet to prevent the hoofs from damaging the lawn.

Some of the landscaped acres over which the mowers clattered were vast. Cyrus Field, famous for laying the first Atlantic cable, had put together a complex that he called Ardsley, extending from Broadway opposite Nevis to the Sawmill River.

Professor McVickar sold his would-be St. Barnabas College property east of Broadway to Mr. Eliphalet Wood, brother of Walter Wood, the inventor and manufacturer of the Wood reaper and mowing machine. Mr. Wood's house was erected in 1869, with its majestic view up and down the Hudson.

To the south of the Wood property was the estate of Frederick Guiteau. Mr. Guiteau seemed to have a special feeling for Irvington. He served its School Board, its Village Board, and years later was the main founder of its public library. It is ironic that when

"Can such things be!" gasped an ecstatic newspaper description of "Ardsley Towers" the home built for his son by Cyrus Field

President Garfield arrived at a Washington railroad station on a July day in 1881 on his way to spend the night with Cyrus Field in Irvington that it was Guiteau's nephew, Charles Guiteau, who assassinated the President.

Albert Bierstadt was one of the best known American artists. For a time Jennie Black's family lived in the Bierstadt mansion on Broadway. She described it:

It stood facing the river, five stories high, with a center tower and two wide balconies outside on the first and second floors on the west and south sides. The north side of the mansion formed the studio, three stories high. This huge studio was about one hundred and fifty feet long by one hundred feet wide. There were four concealed rooms in the wainscoting, half way up the stairs leading to these boxes. The studio was filled with all manner of Indian trophies, Indian costumes, and odd implements of warfare. . . .

An ancient suit of armor stood at each side of the high fireplace, and at one end of the room was a gallery with a big bay window and a window seat. Four years earlier when we were occupying the house, I had used this gallery for a play room. Child that I was when we left there, I can still recall the horror that came over me one day when, from my play gallery, I saw one of those ar-

Fashion changed some houses. The original Guiteau home became . . .

. . . a neo-classic pillared mansion to suit the style of the times. When land values dictated smaller houses the mansion was demolished

The lobby of Ardsley Towers. Alexander the Great or D. W. Griffith could not have done better

mored men walking about the library and realized that he (or it), was clanking up the stairs to my doorway. I shrieked aloud, and was greatly relieved when I heard my brother's voice call out: "Don't be frightened, it's only Ben."

My last vision of this noble house was four years later when I watched it in flames, lighting up the midnight sky for miles around. The three tiers of burning galleries on its two sides gave it a theatrical grandeur and made of it a spectacle impossible to surpass. The entire population of the neighborhood, in varied midnight attire, assembled on the lawns to witness the magnificent sight. The water supply being poor, the building was doomed from the start. In silence we watched as traditions, memories, beauties, flamed skyward and then disappeared forever.

A house becomes a castle. The A. C. Richards house (top) metamorphosed into a castle by Isaac Stern, department store mogul, to follow the turn of the century fashion

One of several "castle-chateaux," built in 1860 by Edmund Coffin, whose own estate was named Repose

"Rochroane," copy of a castle on the Rhine, built by Melchior S. Beltzhoover in 1905

There were castles as well. Travelers back from Europe dubbed the Hudson the American Rhine, and here and there as if on cue castles sprang up on the heights along its shore. Some of the old houses were converted to look like castles, and some were built new. The architect of Irvington's Beltzhoover castle had his instructions to copy his German original to the smallest detail, even to its defects.

There were homes and mansions and castles. A house that is neither a mansion nor a castle but an Irvington landmark is Octagon House. It is also a house with a ghost. Carl Carmer, who lives there, tells the story:

Carl Carmer's Octagon House, built by a member of the Armour meat packing family in 1860; dome and cupola added ten years later

High on the east bank of the Hudson River, and only twenty miles from New York City, stands a strange eight-sided house. It seems to have a park of its own, for it is surrounded by a high hedge in which the bushes were so planted that a number of them bloom in each month from March to October. The park has a unique atmosphere, and anyone who enters it through the winding driveway becomes aware that the trees are of unusual varieties and were planted long ago. Here stand tulip trees, magnolias, maples of Norway and Japan, and a tremendous giant called a "Kentucky Coffee Tree" of a sort which was popular among Hudson Valley residents a hundred years ago. Perhaps the strangest of the trees are the Chinese gingkos, whose leaves in sunlight throw intricate shadows on the green lawn. Since the largest of these stands near the old well-house, which was made in the shape of a Chinese pagoda, the visitor gets a sense of Chinese influence before he reaches the end of the drive. The

house, which is painted in two shades of gray and decorated with white trim, rises five stories high, the last one being a many-windowed cupola which is higher than even the tallest trees. It surmounts a slate-roofed two-storied dome which curves upward from the walls of the second floor. The first floor is circled by a wide veranda bordered by an elaborately designed white wrought-iron railing from which white pillars in groups of three rise to flowered capitals beneath the eaves.

The prosperous merchant to whom this mansion belonged completed it almost a century ago. He was an importer of Chinese teas, and he had recognized in a number of octagon houses then being built (for the building of eight-sided houses was an architectural fad at the time) a similarity to Oriental "summer-houses" which he had seen in his travels beside the lakes and rivers of China. Consequently, many of the designs of the decorations within the house are of Chinese origin, giving it an atmosphere not to be found in any other American dwelling.

The whole place looks as if it had been the scene of a mysterious story. It has been! And it is this story I am about to tell.

When his wife died, the merchant was heartbroken and left the house, which held many happy memories for him. He sold it to a French lady of noble family who, after her husband's death, had brought her only daughter to America. The girl had inherited from her mother great charm and a lively temperament. She was darkly beautiful with black hair and even blacker eyes, and her form was slim and exquisitely modeled.

On a great estate near by lived a rich and aristocratic American family whose ancestors of English blood had lived for several generations in feudal splendor among the "Sugar Islands" off the southern coast of eastern North America. The eldest son of this family had no sooner seen his lovely young neighbor than he fell desperately in love with her. His parents soon discovered that he was making daily visits to the octagonal house whose cupola they could see rising above the hills and trees to the north of their home. Since they had already planned for his marriage to the daughter of another of the great-estate families of the valley, they disapproved of his interest in the French girl and forbade him to see her again.

Though he continued his visits secretly, the girl's mother soon became aware of the situation and, being a person of great family pride herself, ordered her daughter not to see her ardent wooer again. The young couple then took to meeting in a lonely spot on the bank of the river. They soon felt that the restrictions put upon them were intolerable and they planned to run away to New York and be married.

One morning in the spring of the year they met again by the river and hastened to Tarrytown to embark on a steamboat for New York, where they intended to be married. Unhappily for them, a servant of the young man's family saw them hurrying along the riverbank and reported the fact to his employers. At once the father set out in hot pursuit on a spirited horse. In the meantime, his wife ordered her carriage and went to the octagon house, where she upbraided the girl's mother and accused her of conspiring with the lovers.

The pursuing horseman galloped onto the Tarrytown dock just after the gangplank of the steamboat had been drawn aboard.

The steamboat, it developed, was racing against a competitor owned by a rival line. As it entered the shadow of the Palisades, the boiler, which had been subjected to terrific pressure, burst, killing the young man instantly. The steamboat caught fire, and the remaining passengers were soon confronted with the choice of burning to death or attempting to swim from midstream to the shore. That evening when the bodies of the drowned lay upon the river's bank, the corpse of the girl was among them.

The next day a farmer's wagon approached the octagon house bearing a pine box. To the consternation of the driver, however, he was met by an angry woman who bitterly refused to accept his cargo. Eventually the girl was buried in a potter's field near the river.

This should end the story of the fated lovers. Nevertheless, a happenstance—possibly an unrelated coincidence—could be considered by the romantic-minded as having a later bearing upon it.

My wife and I now live in the old octagon house. Twice in recent successive springs my wife has wakened at the end of a strange dream. In it she stands on the moonlit veranda and sees a young girl walking up the drive. She seems to be surrounded by a mellow golden light. Suddenly from the shadows of the veranda darts an older woman, who bars the path of the girl and by stern gestures bids her be gone. The girl wrings her hands and weeps, but her companion is obdurate. At last the girl turns about and, still weeping, walks back whence she came. As she reaches the pagoda-like well-house, she turns about for one last look. As she does so, the other woman beckons to her and opens her arms. The girl begins to run toward her—and the dream ends!

It seems to the present occupants of the house that the two have been reconciled, because whenever we have a visitor who claims to have psychic powers and to understand ghosts, we hear that Octagon House has a special feeling about it—a kind of aura from the past which bears with it a sense of happiness.

Carl Carmer writes a verse from the cupola of his Octagon House:

CUPOLA SONG

When my tower darkens
Climb it slow,
Hear the hounds of Hastings
Give tongue below,

Hear miles upriver,
Swift antiphony,
Echoing choirs at Tarrytown
In full cry:

Black George to Silver Duchess,
And that impetuous pet
Jiggsy belling bald desire
To Yvette.

Then a timeless instant,
Silence—near and far—
Howling hounds soundless,
Stunned by a star!

Carl and Betty Carmer look down from the spiral staircase in the cupola of their Octagon House

Clarence Day who immortalized "Life with Father"

The iceman cometh not

ALTHOUGH IRVINGTON HAD BECOME a traditionally summery place as the 19th century wealthy folk of New York City discovered its pleasures, preparations for summer were not all fun and games. Indeed the village annually braced itself for the invasion of the summer swells.

B y the time the sap was rising in the maples, every available person on the village Main Street was occupied in making the so-called "Big Business" ready in anticipation of the summer residents' arrival. Tradesmen were restocking their shelves. The butcher resurfaced the floor with fresh sawdust and raked attractive designs in it. The druggist returned the unsold fancy goods of the past year to the shelves and display cases. The baggage and expressmen were overtaxed in delivering the many cases of cargo left on the dock by the freight boats. Lawns were fertilized and freshly seeded. Gardens were spaded and made ready for the plants and seedlings that had been started in the greenhouses.

[WEL]

All Irvington merchants were not as cooperative. Clarence Day in his book *Life With Father* records a frustrating experience when the Day family lived in Irvington:

One of the most disgraceful features of life in the country, Father often declared, was the general inefficiency and slackness of small village tradesmen. He said he had originally supposed that such men were interested in business, and that that was why they opened their shops and sunk capital in them, but no, they never used them for anything but gossip and sleep. They took no interest in civilized ways. Hadn't heard of them, probably. He said that of course if he were camping out on the veldt or the tundra, he would expect few conveniences in the neighborhood and would do his best to forego them, but why should he be confronted with the wilds twenty miles from New York?

Usually, when Father talked this way, he was thinking of ice. He strongly objected to spending even one day of his life without a glass of cold water beside his plate at every meal. There was never any difficulty about this in our home in the city. A great silver ice-water pitcher stood on the sideboard all day, and when Father was home its outer surface was frosted with cold. When he had gone to the office, the ice was allowed to melt sometimes, and the water got warmish, but never in the evening, or on Sundays, when Father might want some. He said he liked water, he told us it was one of Nature's best gifts, but he said that like all her gifts it was unfit for human consumption unless served in a suitable manner. And the only right way to serve water was icy cold.

It was still more important that each kind of wine should be served at whatever the right temperature was for it. And kept at it,

90

too. No civilized man would take dinner without wine, Father said, and no man who knew the first thing about it would keep his wine in hot cellars. Mother thought this was a mere whim of Father's. She said he was fussy. How about people who lived in apartments, she asked him, who didn't have cellars? Father replied that civilized persons didn't live in apartments.

One of the first summers that Father ever spent in the country, he rented a furnished house in Irvington on the Hudson, not far from New York. It had a garden, a stable, and one or two acres of woods, and Father arranged to camp out there with many misgivings. He took a train for New York every morning at eight-ten, after breakfast, and he got back between five and six, bringing anything special we might need along with him, such as a basket of peaches from the city, or a fresh package of his own private coffee.

Things went well until one day in August the ice-man didn't come. It was hot, he and his horses were tired, and he hated to come to us anyhow because the house we had rented was perched up on top of a hill. He said afterward that on this particular day he had not liked the idea of making his horses drag the big ice-wagon up that sharp and steep road to sell us fifty cents' worth of ice. Besides, all his ice was gone anyhow—the heat had melted it on him. He had four or five other good reasons. So he didn't come.

Father was in town. The rest of us waited in astonishment, wondering what could be the matter. We were so used to the regularity and punctilio of life in the city that it

seemed unbelievable to us that the ice-man would fail to appear. We discussed it at lunch. Mother said that the minute he arrived she would have to give him a talking to. After lunch had been over an hour and he still hadn't come, she got so worried about what Father would say that she decided to send to the village.

There was no telephone, of course. There were no motors. She would have liked to spare the horse if she could, for he had been worked hard that week. But as this was a crisis, she sent for Morgan, the coachman, and told him to bring up the dog-cart.

The big English dog-cart arrived. Two of us boys and the coachman drove off. The sun beat down on our heads. Where the heavy harness was rubbing on Brownie's coat, he broke out into a thick, whitish lather. Morgan was sullen. When we boys were along he couldn't take off his stiff black high hat or unbutton his thick, padded coat. Worse still, from his point of view, he couldn't stop at a bar for a drink. That was why Mother had sent us along with him, of course, and he knew it.

We arrived at the little town after a while and I went into the Coal & Ice Office. A wiry-looking old clerk was dozing in a corner, his chair tilted back and his chin resting on his dingy shirtfront. I woke this clerk up. I told him about the crisis at our house.

He listened unwillingly, and when I had finished he said it was a very hot day.

I waited. He spat. He said he didn't see what he could do, because the ice-house was

locked.

I explained earnestly that this was the Day family and that something must be done right away.

He hunted around his desk a few minutes, found his chewing tobacco, and said, "Well, sonny, I'll see what I can do about it."

I thanked him very much, as that seemed to me to settle the matter. I went back to the dog-cart. Brownie's check-rein had been unhooked, and he stood with his head hanging down. He looked sloppy. It wouldn't have been so bad with a buggy, but a slumpy horse in a dog-cart can look pretty awful. Also, Morgan was gone. He reappeared soon, coming out of a side door down the street, buttoning up his coat, but with his hat tilted back. He looked worse than the horse.

We checked up the weary animal's head again and drove slowly home. A hot little breeze in our rear moved our dust along with us. At the foot of the hill, we boys got out, to spare Brownie our extra weight. We unhooked his check-rain again. He dragged the heavy cart up.

Mother was sitting out on the piazza. I said the ice would come soon now. We waited.

It was a long afternoon.

At five o'clock, Brownie was hitched up again. The coachman and I drove back to the village. We had to meet Father's train. We also had to break the bad news to him that he would have no ice-water for dinner, and that there didn't seem to be any way to chill his Rhine wine.

The village was as sleepy as ever, but when Father arrived and learned what the situation was, he said it would have to wake up. He told me that he had had a long, trying day at the office, the city was hotter than the Desert of Sahara, and he was completely worn out, but that if any ice-man imagined for a moment he could behave in that manner he, Father, would take his damned head off. He strode into the Coal & Ice Office.

When he came out, he had the clerk with him, and the clerk had put on his hat and was vainly trying to calm Father down. He was promising that he himself would come with the ice-wagon if the driver had left, and deliver all the ice we could use, and he'd be there inside an hour.

Father said, "Inside of an hour be hanged, you'll have to come quicker than that."

The clerk got rebellious. He pointed out that he'd have to go to the stables and hitch up the horses himself, and then get someone to help him hoist a block of ice out of the ice-house. He said it was 'most time for his supper and he wasn't used to such work. He was only doing it as a favor to Father. He was just being neighborly.

Father said he'd have to be neighborly in a hurry, because he wouldn't stand it, and he didn't know what the devil the ice company meant by such actions.

The clerk said it wasn't his fault, was it? It was the driver's.

This was poor tactics, of course, because it wound Father up again. He wasn't interested in whose fault it was, he said. It was everybody's. What he wanted was ice and plenty of it, and he wanted it in time for his dinner. A small crowd which had collected by this time listened admiringly as Father shook his finger at the clerk and said he dined at six-thirty.

The clerk went loping off toward the stables to hitch up the big horses. Father waited till he'd turned the corner.

Followed by the crowd, Father marched to the butcher's.

After nearly a quarter of an hour, the butcher and his assistant came out, unwillingly carrying what seemed to be a coffin, wrapped in a black mackintosh. It was a huge cake of ice.

Father got in, in front, sat on the box seat beside me, and took up the reins. We drove off. The coachman was on the rear seat, sitting back-to-back to us, keeping the ice from sliding out with the calves of his legs. Father went a few doors up the street to a little house-furnishings shop and got out again.

I went in the shop with him this time. I didn't want to miss any further scenes of this performance. Father began proceedings by demanding to see all the man's ice-boxes. There were only a few. Father selected the largest he had. Then, when the sale seemed arranged, and when the proprietor was smiling broadly with pleasure at this sudden windfall, Father said he was buying that refrigerator only on two conditions.

The first was that it had to be delivered at his home before dinner. Yes, now. Right away. The shopkeeper explained over and over that this was impossible, but that he'd have it up the next morning, sure. Father said no, he didn't want it the next morning, he had to have it at once. He added that he dined at six-thirty, and that there was no time to waste.

The shopkeeper gave in.

The second condition, which was then put to him firmly, was staggering. Father announced that that ice-box must be delivered to him full of ice.

The man said he was not in the ice business.

Father said, "Very well then, I don't want it."

The man said obstinately that it was an excellent ice-box.

Father made a short speech. It was the one that we had heard so often at home about the slackness of village tradesmen, and he put such strong emotion and scorn in it that his voice rang through the shop. He closed it by saying, "An ice-box is of no use to a man without ice, and if you haven't the enterprise, the gumption, to sell your damned goods to a customer who wants them delivered in condition to use, you had better shut up your shop and be done with it. Not in the ice business, hey? You aren't in business at all!" He strode out.

The dealer came to the door just as Father was getting into the dog-cart, and called out anxiously, "All right, Mr. Day. I'll get that refrigerator filled for you and send it up right away."

Father drove quickly home. A thunderstorm seemed to be brewing and this had waked Brownie up, or else Father was putting some of his own supply of energy into him. The poor old boy probably needed it as again he climbed the steep hill. I got out at the foot, and as I walked along behind I saw that Morgan was looking kind of desperate, trying to sit in the correct position with his arms folded while he held in the ice with his legs. The big cake was continually slipping and sliding around under the seat and doing its best to plunge out. It had bumped against his calves all the way home. They must have got good and cold.

When the dog-cart drew up at our door, Father remained seated a moment while Morgan, the waitress, and I pulled and pushed at the ice. The mackintosh had come off it by this time. We dumped it out on the grass. A little later, after Morgan had unharnessed and hurridly rubbed down the horse, he ran back to help us boys break the cake up, push the chunks around to the back door, and cram them into the ice-box while Father was dressing for dinner.

Mother was calmed down by this time. The Rhine wine was cooling. "Don't get it too cold," Father called.

Then the ice-man arrived.

The old clerk was with him, like a warden in charge of a prisoner. Mother stepped out to meet them, and at once gave the ice-man the scolding that had been waiting for him all day.

The clerk asked how much ice we wanted. Mother said we didn't want any now. Mr. Day had brought home some, and we had no room for more in the ice-box.

The ice-man looked at the clerk. The clerk tried to speak, but no words came.

Father put his head out of the window. "Take a hundred pounds, Vinnie," he said. "There's another box coming."

A hundred-pound block was brought into the house and heaved into the washtub. The waitress put the mackintosh over it. The ice-wagon left.

Just as we all sat down to dinner, the new ice-box arrived, full.

Mother was provoked. She said, "Really, Clare!" crossly. "Now what am I to do with that piece that's waiting out in the washtub?"

Father chuckled.

She told him he didn't know the first thing about keeping house, and went out to the laundry with the waitress to tackle the problem. The thunderstorm broke and crashed. We boys ran around shutting the windows upstairs.

Father's soul was at peace. He dined well, and he had his coffee and cognac served to him on the piazza. The storm was over by then. Father snuffed a deep breath of the sweet-smelling air and smoked his evening cigar.

"Clarence," he said, "King Solomon had the right idea about these things. 'Whatsoever thy hand findeth to do,' Solomon said, 'do thy damnedest.'"

Mother called me inside. "Whose mackintosh is that?" she asked anxiously. "Katie's torn a hole in the back."

I heard Father saying contentedly on the piazza, "I like plenty of ice."

"Doctor, lawyer, merchant chief"

These were the first stores to be erected in the middle of the block which one sees on the title page of this book. "Poppa" is Constable Raisch (photographed 1893)

The same site in 1900 with a "second generation" of store fronts.

Friberg's shoestore supplied all boots and raincoats for the fire department. At the bottom of the right hand window can be seen one of the earliest ads for S&H Green Stamps

The saloon between the trees on page 95 eventually became Becker's stationery store, still the center of gravity of Irvington's business section. As with most businesses in the village about this time, second story dwellings were added

Peter Laffan's paint business prospered, moving from a shack-like structure to elegant premises across the street and stressing, instead of paper hanging, fresco painting. Old and young codgers enjoyed sitting on the ledge in front of his store

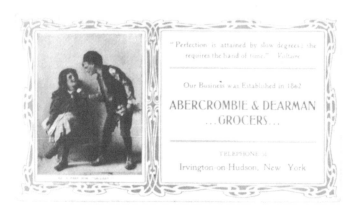

This grocery market thrived in the 90's though across the street from the grander Abercrombie and Dearman competition

The same store a decade earlier with customers waiting to get next to the pot-bellied stove

Two views of the Abercrombie and Dearman property. The taller building was Irvington's first bank. Abercrombie was sometime president of the village. Dearman was a direct descendant of Justus, founder of the village. Once a week, when the wholesale food barge docked at Irvington, a whistle blew and all the grocers' carts held a break-neck race to have first choice of the comestibles

The Irvington Hotel extends a warm welcome—guest with raised glass, attentive staff, convenient horsetrough and kennel and a reassuring supply of kegs fronting the hostelry

Mr. Wistrand is the gentleman in shirtsleeves. He immigrated from Sweden to practice his craft among well-dressed Irvingtonians

Petri's market of the '90's. The merchandise is forcefully displayed, including garlands on the lighting fixtures and meat hooks. Meat was chosen in the city. It was then stamped, hung for six weeks and delivered to the store's "ice safe" from which the daily supply was brought forth

The laundry, like the other retail and service businesses in the village, existed principally to cater to the whims and needs of the great estates

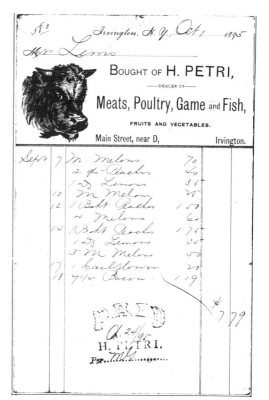

101

"The Asphalt King," white-mustachioed Amzi Lorenzo Barber, pictured here with his family. Realizing what the development of the automobile and the subsequent demand for good roads would mean to his company he was one of the first to sponsor the new horseless carriage

George Washington Hill with his son, Percival S. Hill, 2nd. Advertising genius and the maker of Lucky Strikes, he revolutionized American smoking habits. His home in Irvington had tobacco plants in the flower beds

Holder's Baggage Express, photographed in front of Ackerman's tinsmithing shop. The Holders were among the early merchant families in the village

Schneiders's saloon, in full bunting for the "4th." This was one of seven saloons owned by seven widows in Irvington

Will Morris, Arthur Beswick and Frank Lord, prescription fillers at Barr's drugstore which still functions as the Irvington Pharmacy

Irvington News.
Irvington-on-Hudson, N. Y.

F. H. MORRELL, Local Representative

Entered temporarily as second class matter at the post office at Irvington-on-Hudson, N. Y.

Issued every Saturday

THE GAZETTE
IRVINGTON

A Community Newspaper Devoted to the Activities, Interests and News
of the People of Irvington and the Town of Greenburgh

Masthead of Irvington's first newspaper, the "News," and colophon of the "Gazette," founded in 1907 and published weekly until 1969

Dr. Fulton, local physician, became health officer in 1874 when a case of small-pox was discovered. The more than 600 residents were promptly vaccinated

LORD & BURNHAM CO.

HORTICULTURAL ARCHITECTS & BUILDERS,
STEAM & HOT WATER HEATING ENGINEERS.

Irvington on Hudson, N.Y. DEC. 3, *1891*

For Lord and Burnham, the village's first industry, the making of boilers and greenhouses was a logical combination. The plant, pictured also on the cover of the book, was erected entirely on filled land that changed the shoreline of the river

The "Behrens block," erected speculatively address by address, from 98 to 108 Main Street, beginning in 1905. Ernest Behrens, grandson of the builder, has lived in every one of the flats

TO·NIGHT

Feb. 1-1912

THE NEW WISTRAND HALL OPENS

FEBRUARY 1st, 1912

MOTION PICTURES AND ~~ ILLUSTRATED SONGS

To Our Patrons:

It is the purpose of the management to conduct this theatre in such a way that at all times the influence of the show will educate the young; interest the adults and abstain in every way from features that are not of a high order and at the same time be strictly up-to-date. The Pictures will be changed every day and the songs twice a week.

Hours: 4 to 6 P. M. and 8 to 10 P. M.

Admission: 5 and 10 Cents

∴ TO·NIGHT ∴

GAZETTE 10 PRINT

Feb'y 1-1912
Thursday.

With a change of show every day, it must have been "up-to-date"

Relatively unchanged in 80 years except for the traffic which in the '90's moved on the "wrong side" of the street. Contrary to the postcard's information, the view looks east!

Irvington's most elegant business structure. Designed by Stanford White and resembling a domeless National Capitol, it housed the Cosmopolitan magazine from 1895 to 1904. Its famous editor and publisher, Arthur Brisben Walker, lived in Irvington

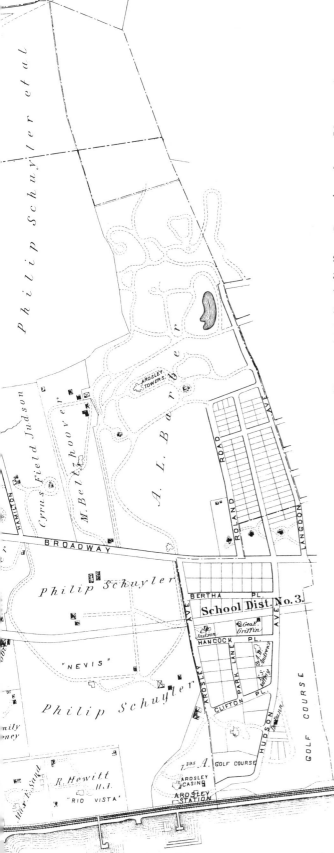

Winter sports

"WINTER SPORTS were our great pleasure," Jennie Black writes:

The sleighing parties with their great sleighs, overladen with fur rugs, so spacious as to accommodate eight or ten persons with comfort. The horses dressed in holiday attire with silver bells and great red plumes. The hitching on behind of the youngsters, all off for a real party.

Then the coasting; old and young met together with every conceivable kind of sled, from the small coasters to the great bob sleds.

Many of the lanes were open for coasting from Broadway to the Hudson River, and the sight of young and old all joining in this exhilarating, though often dangerous, sport was a picture never to be forgotten.

Irving Lane, or Sunnyside Lane, was the favored of all the coasting thoroughfares, especially on moonlit nights. On darker nights, and for special parties, this lane was equipped with great torches at dangerous points to illuminate the way. For the trip up the hill, a horse was waiting below to bring back the heavy bobs and anyone who found the walk too laborious.

The Great Estate Era—1901

Sleighing party in the style of 1869

At ten o'clock in the evening, the party started for some house to which they had been invited. How grateful it was, after the extreme cold, to come back to a blazing fireplace.

Isabel Benjamin gives her account of winter fun:

There was plenty of ice and snow in those days. We coasted on our own sleds and on the bobsleds of the men who steered them.

We had one long coast from the top of Stern's hill across Broadway (as all sleighs stopped for us to pass), down Tiffany Lane to the river. Mr. Howard Jaffray often brought his horses to draw our sleds up the hill.

I loved hitching. It was fun to tie a rope to the front of the sled, run at the side of a moving sleigh, or preferably a delivery truck, throw the end of rope around the axle of the sleigh holding the other end and generally land flat on one's tummy on the sled. Then off to Tarrytown or Dobbs Ferry.

Once I had forgotten to deliver in the kitchen fresh eggs for which I had been sent to the chicken house. They were in the pocket of a nice English coat I wore! I remember my mother's horror when, after hitching, I returned home, and she looked at my coat!

———————

Barton Eddison was born in Irvington "just after Rip Van Winkle," as he puts it. Engineer, inventor, sportsman, raconteur, he reminisces:

An intrepid snowshoer

About the turn of the century they built a wooden toboggan chute every winter, that ran from North Mountain down almost to Broadway. It went across on a trestle high enough for a horse and carriage to pass under, over Osceola Avenue and the pond below. We ended in a meadow—sometimes right side up and sometimes not. In those days they didn't believe in "lifts"—we got our exercise pulling the toboggans back up. On a good day there were a great many broken elbows! . . . We started skiing here about 1910. That was pretty early for skiing in this country. Irvington was *avant garde* as usual. We skied down North Mountain where the old toboggan slide used to be . . . We used to race cars on the Hudson River when it was frozen. We had chains on our tires, of course. I used to fire up my Stanley Steamer and join in. I'd take on all comers. Once Pathé News came to photograph a race. When I saw the picture there were four little black dots on the ice. Suddenly

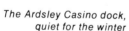
Blizzard on Main Street

one had a white plume, and the other dots disappeared in the steam. That was my Stanley Steamer.

———————

But one winter a storm overshadowed sports. Isabel Benjamin wrote:

On the morning of the historic blizzard in 1888, my mother would not allow me to go to town. Later we learned that the train I wanted to take, leaving Irvington at 8:08, reached New York on the following morning. Some passengers got off and plowed through the snow to safety. Others ate the eggs and drank the milk being sent to New York by the families who had Irvington homes, and spend winters in town.

The Ardsley Casino dock, quiet for the winter

Chicken salad al fresco

And summer

OF IRVINGTON SUMMERS JENNIE BLACK RE-CALLS:

As winters were severe, our summers were often furiously warm. Before the days of wire screens a mosquito net hung over every bed. How well I recall stifling nights under those nets which prevented even a breath of air from reaching one's anatomy! My most treasured companions of the night were a bottle of camphor and a large palm leaf fan.

Still our summers were full of charm. Archery, croquet, garden and yachting parties

The Sporting Life; croquet on the lawn

A commuter's yacht off the Casino dock

filled the social calendar. Several of these yachts were sufficiently large to cross the Atlantic, and most of them steamed off each morning with their owners and a company of friends [from Irvington] to New York City, returning in the late afternoon.

About 1880 tennis was brought into our village through the Howard Jaffray family. This tennis caused great excitement and was a real novelty.

Bowling and bicycles and the new golf were much in style. Barton Eddison recalls going into New York for lessons in bicycling at Spaulding's, "because no one knew how to ride the new 'safeties', as they were called."

Above all Irvington people loved to ride and drive.

Tennis was popular the year around in Irvington—the costume suited the season

Bicycling was popular too . . .

Ladies properly clothed in riding habits sat side saddle on their mounts and competed with an occasional troop of Cavalry or Battery of Artillery that added to the show. The noise of hoof, chains, wheels and equipment at times interrupted the church services as they passed by.

Jennie Black continues:

A picturesque sight on Broadway was the afternoon drive. There were vehicles of all descriptions from the one horse buggy to the four horse coach with silver and brass mounted harness and coachmen with dark blue coats, high hats, white gloves and pat-

. . . And coaching

Coach and Four carried Irvington passengers north on Broadway to Tarrytown and South to Yonkers

Jaffray boys, with their goat cart, on Main Street. John Barr, druggist, in white coat

ent leather boots with pink tops. Many children owned either a pony or a donkey that could be hitched to small carts or phaetons. Anything that would go steadily and keep in line could join the procession. At a given signal, away we went, each keeping behind the other, and after a trip about the neighborhood would return in like manner for some light refreshments.

There were humbler drivers as well. Isabel Benjamin was one:

. . . I had a goat, as did Fanny Cottenet. We drove them together. My father gave me a sulky, so Billy the goat and I raced the coaches which gentlemen sports drove through Irvington every week in the summer.

Typical vehicles seen in Irvington around the turn of the century. On the left, a side-bar road wagon; on the right, an open landau

A rubbernecker-doubledecker excursion carriage

"A pleasance of midas"

THE NINETIES WERE GAY—and nowhere gayer than in Irvington. New York's 400 had found a new playground.

Journalist Elizabeth Cushman writing of the '90's said:

"The finest lawn tennis courts in metropolitan New York"

The first country club to excite the entire United States and to create a standard of social excellence never exceeded opened in May of 1896.

Its existence, heralded widely in the metropolitan press of the day, was irrefutable proof that here, in Westchester, was gath-

ered the cream of the country's society. It was additional proof of the fact that the wealthiest spot of ground in the world, in proportion to its population, lay between Sleepy Hollow and Irvington. General Philip Schuyler, who occupied Nevis, was president of the club; Amzi L. Barber, who

The Ardsley Casino boasted its own station, matching the Club architecture, on the main line of the New York Central

brought one of the first automobiles to this county, was vice president; Cyrus Field Judson, grandson of Cyrus Field, was secretary; and General Samuel Thomas was treasurer.

The Board of Governors included John D. Rockefeller, William Rockefeller, William S. Webb, Henry Villard, John Pierpont Morgan, Cornelius Vanderbilt, and Chauncey DePew. . . .

[It was] a center where the socially and financially great throughout the East gathered in all their grandeur. The press called them "swells" in those days, distinguished between the different grades by noting that one was "plain" swell while the next was a "howling" swell. Plain and howling alike, however, all were listed on the roster of this first great golf club in Westchester—the Ardsley Casino, now known as the Ardsley Club. . . .

Golf and the Ardsley Club were new together. The first Summer that the Club was opened there was a famous match played on the links between Willie Dunn and Willie Park, both professionals. It took place on August 8, when the thermometer hovered around 100. Golf balls in those days were made of gutta percha—and gutta percha softens in heat. One smart crack from a club and the ball simply became a pulp. However, the ingenious players were prepared for the emergency. They carried their golf balls around on ice! Willie Park's caddy had a tin bucket wrapped in a towel, much as a champagne bucket might be; Willie Dunn's had put both the ice and the balls in an old leather satchel which per-

What the well dressed golfing girl wore on the Ardsley links in 1890

spired profusely as the game progressed and the ice melted. The press was filled with admiration for this notable notion, though the day was not yet over when disparaging comments about this ridiculous game where grown men chased little balls across whole cow pastures, had ceased.

There were women on the Ardsley links even in those long-ago days. At first, though the fair sex had been given a cordial welcome to the club house, they restricted their activities to sitting around the piazzas. . . .

The ladies did not sit very long however. By 1898, the women's golf champion of America had won her title on the Ardsley links.

THE FOUR HORSE COACH

PIONEER

Will run during the Spring Season, 1895,

Commencing Monday, April 15th
BETWEEN

NEW YORK AND WESTCHESTER

via Harlem, Washington Bridge, Jerome Park, Fordham, Bronxdale, Williams-Bridge,
Westchester and the Country Club, LEAVING the

HOTEL BRUNSWICK, NEW YORK. at 11 A.M.
DAILY, (SUNDAYS EXCEPTED), AND

COUNTRY CLUB, - at 4.00 P. M., arriving in New York at 6.00 P.M.

This Coach stops to Take Up and Set Down Passengers anywhere on the Road, EXCEPT Between the Hotel Brunswick and Plaza Hotel, 59th St.

FARE, $2.50.   BOX SEAT, $1.00 Extra.

PASSENGERS' LUGGAGE up to 50 lbs. FREE.   PARCELS carried at
MODERATE RATES, and punctually delivered anywhere on the road.

SEATS may be secured in the Office of the Hotel Brunswick or Plaza Hotel, on and after April 1st.

N. B.—PASSENGERS CAUTIONED TO BE ON TIME.

Coach
and four

COACHING WAS POPULAR in the early 1900's. A coach was driven from New York City to the Ardsley Casino with dramatic flourish and liveried footmen in the high "rumble seat." Barton Eddison recalls it:

The coach was driven up on Saturdays from the Holland House in the city by one of the Vanderbilts. It was a four-in-hand— and members bought tickets to come up to the Casino. There were five changes of horses along the way, to keep the pace fast, and a blast from a footman's horn warned of the approaching coach so that the fresh

"Off for the Ardsley Club . . ." The Vanderbilt coach and four leaves Holland House in New York City. Passengers paid extra for outside seats.

Horse drinking trough on peaceful Broadway, 1907. End of an era

team of horses would be waiting . . . I can recall that when I was a schoolboy a Saturday event was watching the coach go by on Broadway. You would hear the French horn from the fellow in the rumble seat and then the four-in-hand would come roaring by. They had the last change of horses in Hastings so they were at full speed when they turned down the Casino drive.

The horseless carriage

THE FIRST AUTOMOBILE snorted and backfired its way up Broadway with as much noise as the old *Clermont* chuffing up the Hudson— and wrought even more dramatic changes in the leisurely traffic of the old Post Road.

Jennie Black describes her first auto ride:

One day my husband's brother, John, drove into our gateway with the queerest looking contraption I had ever seen. It looked like a sort of a buggy without a horse, shaft or whiffletree, and without a top. Of course, I had heard and read about the "horseless carriages," but I had never seen one. This oddity at our front door turned out to be the first mobile on general

The electric automobile, dawn of a new age

119

All bundled up for a midday muddy drive

sale, and I believe it was the first to come through our village.

I can never forget my sensation as I climbed up into my seat and we began to move forward. I felt sure I would fall over the dashboard at the slightest provocation. I said, "Please don't go up on Broadway—I feel so silly perched up here without a horse."

In those days all the engine was underneath the seat. We could *see* nothing but the road in front as we went along. So we went up Dublin way and fared much worse than had we stayed on Broadway. All the dogs in that section—and there were many—came out to tell us what they thought about it, and some of the old-time loiterers at Hall's Corner called out, "Get a horse." Many of the boys made jeering remarks. One fired a stone that came perilously near my head.

As we turned a sudden corner we saw com-

ing toward us a farmer and his wife in a buggy, with an old white mare. I shall never forget what followed when the horse caught sight of us. Without warning she stopped, sat down in the middle of the road with her two front feet firmly planted, her hind legs coming out between, her ears cocked forward, her eyes bulging, fright in every pore of her emaciated frame. As she was in the middle of the road, we could not pass, for the road was narrow with a steep ditch on either side. My brother-in-law stopped the car, and there we stood looking at one another, the horse snorting, the farmer swearing.

"Can't you give us a little room?" said my brother-in-law in a persuasive voice.

"Go to h---!" was the farmer's only answer.

Irvington's only underpass (the tunnel under the aqueduct), intimidating to horse—or automobile

120

Samuel Davis, father of the Locomobile, with family and driver prepare for a run. "A tremendous breeze was created at 15 miles an hour."

We decided, instead of following his un-friendly advice, to back the car. So back we did. We backed and backed until we struck a crossroad. Meanwhile we saw in the distance the farmer trying with one hand to restrain his frightened wife from climbing out of the buggy, while with the other he endeavored to induce the terrified animal to resume her natural position. We wended our way home from the White Plains Road to Broadway and I heaved a sigh of relief and thanked God with fervor when we reached the front door of our home in safety.

————

Barton Eddison vividly remembers the "new contraption":

About 1903 we had one of the first automobiles in Irvington. It was a Curved-Dash Oldsmobile with a four and a half horse-power single cylinder engine under the body. It steered with a tiller and had nothing but kerosene sidelights and no top— but we could go on the level about 25 miles an hour. Up a hill like Harriman Road you would shift to low gear and chug up—and four or five dogs would usually run circles around you . . . Father had bought a car before that—in 1901—but we never saw it. He had ordered a Locomobile Steamer and paid a deposit of $100. He was notified that the car was in New York. "Before I take it," he said, "I'd like to see how this is fired up —cold." So they showed him. He walked out and said, "You can keep the $100."

Locomobile at pasture

Jennie Black looked at the new way the world would move:

Of course, the auto has come to stay and we could never be happy without it, but oh, for one of those old-time "runaways" with the horses tearing down Broadway, everyone running as if to a fire, and then the final smash-up sooner or later—often with results too serious for any possible amusement. But a good old-fashioned buggy runaway is nevertheless a country reminiscence that must ever bring a thrill. Just as was the old-time country fire, with the horses and engines racing up the road at two in the morning.

———

A grace note on early automobiling is supplied by the always adventurous Isabel Benjamin:

When I bought my first little Dodge car a young man from the garage where I got it gave me two lessons. I nearly landed us on the railroad tracks, and I smashed the policeman's signal lantern. The following day another young man came. When I asked about my first instructor, he said that "at the garage they thought it better to send an unmarried man."

Aerial view of Irvington, 1958. Automobile highways have created a new landscape

Family album

A PORTRAIT OF A VILLAGE includes faces. Musya Sheeler (Mrs. Charles Sheeler) photographed some of her neighbors with perception and wit in the 1940's and '50's. Selections of her art make up an Irvington family album.

Robert B. Greig Smith. In his retirement he often sat on his porch on Main Street with his favorite parrot which greeted friends, "Hello Sweetheart!"

Albert Newman, hack driver from the horse and buggy days. He walked his rooster on a leash. The pet's claws were painted with bright red nail polish

John A. Buckhout, custodian of the Town Hall, great grandson of Captain John who was featured in Ripley's "Believe It Or Not" as leaving, at the age of 103 years, 240 descendents

Miss Daisy Rutter pours from her Georgian silver teapot. Among her treasures is a lock of George Washington's hair given as a wedding present to her mother by Alexander Hamilton's son

Patsy Gemma, born in Avellino, Italy, worked from 1925 with the Irvington highway department. He is pictured proud in his decoration of the park for Memorial Day

Walter H. McNeilly, mail carrier in Irvington for 46 years

Mrs. Joseph G. Mattison, who lived to be 101 years old, was given the family china by her 90 year old aunt. In the presence of visitors the china cabinet often gave a loud "crack," to which she replied, "Oh, that is only Aunt Gusta speaking her mind."

The artist's eye

Unique among 19th century American painters, Albert Bierstadt (1830–1902) rendered panoramic scenes from the far west and the east. His Irvington home, the "Glorious . . . outcropping of Mr. Bierstadt" is pictured here with one of his famous oils—A view of the Merced river, Yosemite valley

Cuban nude, 36 x 59 in. oil painting

Bernard Karfiol (1886–1952). Born in Budapest of American parents, he became a close friend and neighbor of Charles Sheeler. His paintings are represented in many of America's leading museums. His work is characterized by tenderness and sensuous form

This Karfiol painting was acquired as a memorial to Alice E. Tewey, teacher at the Irvington elementary school

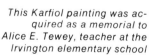

127

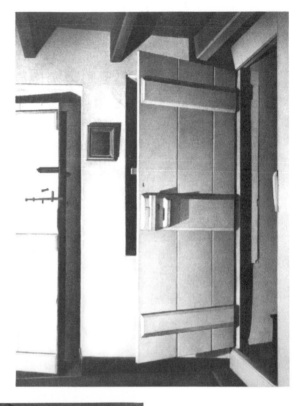

Charles Sheeler (1883–1965), artist in the American tradition, discoverer of the industrial subject. Sheeler is perhaps most interesting in that he could see all of America in the shape and setting of a Bucks County barn. He was also among the truly modern photographers

These two works are typical of his cool simplification in planes and masses. Top, Open Door, 1932. Below, Composition Around White, 1959

The Sketch Book

ONE OF WASHINGTON IRVING'S best-known works was his Sketch Book. Here is a respectful echo—bits and pieces from his village.

A hermit
and a
lonely grave

JOHANN STOLTING was a familiar figure as he walked along Irvington's streets during the 1880's. His clothes he had made himself. His shoes were little more than sandals. No one remembered that he ever wore a hat of any sort. He was fond of children and they were fond of him, and he was not unsociable with the few neighbors who shared the hillside on which he had built his cabin overlooking the Saw Mill River Valley.

No one knows for sure of his past. He is said to have been born on Heligoland where he spent his youth. He was well educated and migrated to this country and for a time taught languages.

Whatever the reasons, his eccentricities grew. He provided for the few necessities of life by turning out wooden buttons that he made on a homemade lathe that he operated by foot power, and sold the product around the village.

He was also a familiar figure on the banks of the Saw Mill and Hudson Rivers where he went for his daily bath, even in winter. If the ice did not stop him, he never missed a day. Sometimes, for the sport of it, he would climb aboard an hospitable ice cake in the Hudson River and sail along the banks wherever the current took him.

He had found the life that suited him and he was foresighted enough to ensure that its end would be as he would have it. He had his own coffin made of local chestnut wood and used it as his bed for a number of years before it assumed its eternal function.

His grave is only a few hundred feet west of the Saw Mill River Parkway, which was deliberately swerved in the vicinity to avoid disturbing it—the only marked grave in the village of Irvington.

A drawing and a rubbing of Stolting's remote grave

JOHANN W. STOLTING.
NATIVE OF THE ISLE
HELIGOLAND.
BORN 1810.
DIED JAN. 10. 1888.

129

Political high life

POLITICS CAME AND POLITICIANS WENT, but in 1890 at least the Democratic Committee of the Town of Greenburgh was living high. The annual dinner menu read:

HUITRES.
En Coquille.   Sauterne.

SOUPS.
Crême à la Reine.   Amontilado.

HORS D'OEUVRES.
Variés.

POISSONS
Salmon de Kennebec, Sauce Hollandaise.
Cucumber Salad.   Barsac.

RELEVES.
Filet of Beef, Piqué aux Champignons.
Pommes Parisiennes.
Haricot Vert.   St. Estephe.

ENTREES.
Sweetbreads Moderne.

LEGUMES
Asparagus, Cream Sauce.

PUNCH.
Cleopâtra

ROTIS,
Canvas Back Ducks, Currant Jelly.
Quails on Toast, au cresson.
Mayonnaise de Celery.   Pomery sec,
                                 Perrier Jouet.

ENTREMETS SUCRES,
Babas au Rum.

DESSERT.
Ice Cream, fancy forms.
Petits Fours. Bonbons.
Candied Fruits.
Fancy Mottoes. Fruits.
Fromage.

CAFÉ NOIR,
Creme de Menthe. Cognac. Chatreuse.

One of America's great black tycoons, Madame C. J. Walker was also a noted philanthropist

Millionairess

IN 1907 SARAH J. WALKER was a hard working Negro laundress glad to earn $1.50 a day doing "family wash." She had been born, some forty years earlier, in Delta, Louisiana. She died, in 1919, the wealthiest woman of her race, and left, beside her fortune, a mansion, "Villa Lewaro," which she had built on Broadway in Irvington over some vigorous local objections and furnished at an expense of "in excess of $350,000."

In the intervening years between laundress and millionairess Sarah Walker, by then known as Madame Walker, had invented, patented, and brilliantly market-managed the "anti-kink" lotion to straighten Negro hair. She established beauty salons, advertised her products widely, and kept a canny control of her company's finances.

How Madame Walker and her elaborate household entourage were received in Irvington (nor how she wished to be received) is

Madame Walker's Villa Lewaro, named for Lelia Walker Robinson by the owner's friend, Enrico Caruso, was the "cultural capital of black America." Now a home for "Companions of the Forest," the mansion still commands northern Broadway in Irvington

not recorded. On her death newspaper headlines called her the richest Negro woman. She was also one of the first and most astute women business executives of any race.

Later headlines, when her daughter sold "Villa Lewaro" in 1930, provide an ironic footnote to Sarah Walker's spectacular success:

MME WALKER'S PALACE FINERY SOLD
AT AUCTION

FURNISHINGS OF LATE INVENTOR
OF HAIR TONIC BRINGING LITTLE

GLORY THAT WAS MADAME WALKER'S
PROVIDES OPTICAL ORGY
FOR CURIOUS WHITE FOLK

VALUABLES BOUGHT BY THOSE WHO
OPPOSED MANSION ON THE HUDSON

The Whitecap Committee

MADAME WALKER WAS NOT the only object of local discrimination:

Irvington, July 8th, 1892

Mr. Isaac Stearn
Sir,
We wrote to you about 7 or 8 days ago about those Itilians [*sic*] and it seems you laughed at it. Well now we want them and the man that is over them Con. Kennedy discharged tomorrow night or suffer the consequences. I should think Mr. Knapper knew better than to bring them on the place. We will give him a call before it is

swimming pool at the Gould mansion Lyndhurst:

I ran across the lawn, following little hand-printed signs which read "Swimming pool . . . use gravel path." In the center of a grove of cedar trees I came upon a large red brick building with Doric columns flanking the portico.

Immediately inside was a foyer with dressing rooms on either side . . . Men on the right . . . Ladies to the left. Straight ahead was the swimming pool. I had expected to see something more elaborate than "the old swimming hole," but not the largest indoor body of water in the United States! I wondered if it was high or low tide?

Immense columns surrounding the pool upheld a sky-lighted ceiling. The lower half of the columns were painted cinnamon red; the rest was pure white. Between the col-

all over. This is the last so you can do as you think best and if this is not heeded you will hear from us personally.

Yours Respectfully,
WHITECAP COMMITTEE

"High or low tide?"

HELEN GOULD SHEPARD's daughter-in-law, Celeste Seton, described her first visit to the

The great dining hall at Lyndhurst, designed by Alexander Jackson Davis, left by Jay Gould's daughter to the National Trust

Searching for the lifeguard at Lyndhurst

umns were pots of tall tropical palms and life preservers were carefully hung at equal intervals around the pool.

Far out in the middle of this great expanse of water was a lifeboat, and resting on the oars was a good-looking, blonde young man. His occupation was stamped in large block letters across his jersey: "Lifeguard." He was passing the time of day throwing a rubber ball to half a dozen dogs who frantically swam after it. "The cocker spaniel always gets it," he yelled, as he heaved it again half way down the pool.

Olivia [Mrs. Shepard's daughter] appeared wearing a one-piece bathing suit and, to my surprise, a pair of black stockings.

"I'll run in and change," I said. I came out a moment later and was about to plunge in when Olivia cried: "Celeste,—wait a moment, please. You have no stockings on." I turned around a little bewildered.

"Mother never lets us go in without stockings," Olivia said.

"Without stockings!" I said incredulously.

"Yes, it's an absolute rule."

"I'm sorry. I didn't know. It seems rather old fashioned."

"It's from the Bible," Olivia explained. "Some chapter in Deuteronomy, I think. But don't worry, I have an extra pair. I'll get them for you."

The tale of a fountain

IN FRONT OF THE VILLAGE HALL there stands a beautiful marble fountain that has long since ceased to serve its original function as a watering spot for horses, with a low trough for dogs. Around its edge are the words "Blessed are the merciful for they shall obtain mercy, February 16, 1889."

The fountain was a memorial to a well-loved doctor of the village, Isaiah Ashton, who was killed when his horse bolted and the carriage overturned. Geraniums now grace his memorial.

See page 119 for the original site of the fountain

Rough Riders

THE WAR OF 1898 with Spain had its echo in Irvington. Barton Eddison remembers:

One of my pet recollections was seeing my hero Teddy Roosevelt after the Spanish-American War. He and his Rough Riders came up Broadway on horseback. The whole village turned out to line the street! I found a good place perched on top of one of the stone pillars at a driveway entrance and saw Teddy go by—with his teeth and his glasses . . . He was always my hero.

Paulding's leg

[WEL]

On July 3, 1877 the southbound Chicago Express ran into an open switch just south of the Irvington depot, and several of the cars overturned into the Hudson. The site has been filled in and buildings of Lord and Burnham have been erected upon it. Four persons were killed and several others were injured. They were treated in neighboring homes by doctors Todd and Pooley of Dobbs Ferry. A gentleman by the name of Paulding had a leg so badly crushed that it was necessary to amputate. The operation was performed in a home on North "B" Street. The severed leg was taken to an empty lot on the corner of South "B" Street and Main, according to a newspaper clipping.

The following is a bit of folklore pertaining to the above incident. Several weeks after the wreck, a gentleman with one leg drove down Main Street and asked some bystanders if they knew where the leg was buried. He was directed to the spot where they helped him exhume the leg. He explained that he was suffering considerably and hoped that if he gave it a proper burial he would be relieved of the discomfort.

Irvington beech. Photograph by Charles Sheeler

Woodman
spare that tree

TREES HAVE ALWAYS GRACED IRVINGTON. The venerable oaks and maples, the arching elms, the glowing copper beeches have been as much a part of the village as the people who lived beneath them. Long before the word "conservationist" was heard of trees were sometimes threatened.

Jennie Black describes one encounter:

One day Mr. Howard Jaffray, staunch friend of our Village, came along with one of his sons and saw a number of men carrying large saws, standing on Broadway in front of an eccentric gentleman's residence.

"What are you doing here?" asked Mr. Jaffray. "Well," announced the foreman of the gang, "Mr. X wants the tops of these trees taken off so that he can see the river from his porch."

As these were the most magnificent trees on our main highway, Mr. Jaffray was justly incensed. "Never on your life," he cried. "If you touch one of these trees, I will shoot you." Whereupon he dispatched his son for a rifle, and calmly took his post as watchman on Mr. X's stone wall. The gun being on his knees and he ready for action, our lovely trees were saved.

Cyrus and Mary Field, 1885, on the porch of Ardsley, their "Homestead," painted a fashionable dark red

The birth
of a bank

IT WAS A COMFORTABLE June afternoon in 1881 when a distinguished threesome of Jay Gould, Cyrus Field, and Ogden Bradley were sitting on the porch of Field's house. They were planning a reception for President James A. Garfield who was to be Mr. Field's houseguest.

The conversation was suddenly interrupted. Four armed men with revolvers and shotguns dismounted from a carriage and hurried toward the porch.

Mr. Field was the only one of the three who took this calmly. He explained that the payroll for people working on his estate had to be brought in, in cash, under close guard, since there was no bank between Yonkers and Ossining, and very few local merchants were willing to cash checks.

Leaving off plans for a Presidential reception, the three gentlemen immediately began assessing the potential profits of founding a bank. Mr. Bradley, who had recently retired, took the major responsibility. Within six weeks, capital of one hundred thousand dollars had been raised and the Westchester County Savings Bank was a reality.

Perhaps the definitive comment on Jay Gould and Cyrus Field was made by the Reverend William Henry Benjamin, for forty years before his death in 1907 rector of St. Barnabas Church. Arriving at his dentist's office one day, he was asked how he was feeling and he replied cheerfully, "As well as anyone could be expected to who lives halfway between Cyrus Field and Jay Gould."

The Field-Gould relationship deteriorated. Gould ruine
Field financially. A final spite appears on the map—
Gould's plan (unrealized) to route an extension of th
rapid transit line through Field's esta

SUNNY SIDE
Washington Irving Est.
E. S. Jaffray 1814
SCHOOL
SUNNYSIDE LANE
H. Parish 8 a.
T.A.Strong
H. Parish 21 a.
PETER BONT ROAD
F.M.
PRESB. PARSONAGE
Mrs. W.H.Fogg
Cunningham Est. 21 a.
J. C. Fargo 38 a.
E. Lyle Co. 3 a.
Dr. E. Prince
C.C.Worthington
M.R.Bishop 11 a.
H.R.Bishop "CRAIG HALL"
Geo. D. Morgan
72 a. Geo. D. Morgan
Starr
F.B.Perkins
Geo. A. Blood
"WOOD CLIFF"
"STRAWBERRY HILL" 28 a.
F. O. Matthiessen 43 a.
W. Barton Est. 48 a.
50 a. Est.
"RIDGE VIEW"
40 a.
C. L. Tiffany 19 a.
"TIFFANY PARK"
PRES B. CH.
ST. BARNABAS P. E. CH.
R. C. CH.
A. C. Richard
Formerly Isaac Stern
"IRVING CLIFF" 50
40 a.
Rockwood
R. R. STATION
Mill
St. House Waters Prop.
IRVINGTON
Merrick MAIN ST.
Anderson
Eliphalet Wood 52 a.
McCat
F.W. Guiteau
Harriman 5 a.
ARDSLEY
REDWOOD Lord & Burnham
"HILLSIDE"
Dr. Carroll Dunham 6 384/1000
F. W. Guiteau
J. H. Whitehouse 12 a.
J. H. Whitehouse 34 a.
PARK AVE.
F.W. Emory
D. N. Barney Est. 17 a.
A. L. Barney 6½
S. S. Rubira
"EL RETIRO"
A. J. Mannay
Spring Brook
Dr. Wm. I. Drake Est.
A. B. Eidelt 3½ a.
Mrs. E. G. Gregory 7 a.
Supt W. Murray
16 a.
Ardsley 38
Chas. Palliser
E. H. Mairs 8¼ a.
"GELNAIRN"
424/1000
Dr. Lucian Warner
"CROMONT"
"THE MAPLE" S.S.Goodsman
S. S. Goodman
E.P.Claggett
PROSPECT HILL
Palliser
J. D. Mairs Est. "LYNNWOOD" 9 a.
Wm. H. Preston
SUNNYSIDE PARK
G. Palliser
Palliser
G. Palliser
"CHARLTON HALL" David Dows Est. 27 a.
Geo. W. Smith 6 a.
209 Miss R. Wendell
Miss R. Wendell 11 a.
Miss R. Wendell 20 a.
H. Cannon
Harper Butler
G. Palliser
COMPANY
Ellsworth
CLINTON AVE.
W. F. Cary Jr. Est.
Geo. W. Dibble
"BEACH LAWN" Mrs. Fletcher Harper 9 a.
WOODLANDS
HUDSON
F. A. Foster
H. H. Cannon 6 a.
Mrs. T. W. Walters "NEARWOOD" 14 a.
MAIRS Est. DOWS Est.
D. Dows Jr. 11 a.
"NEVIS"
180
CROTON AQUEDUCT
A. Hamilton Est.
Mrs. L. D. Cooksey
PROPOSED
Hampden Est.
MIDLAND
SAW MILL RIVER
"ARDSLEY"
Cyrus W. Field
M.R. Field
"INNANDA"
E.M. Field
Mrs. D.A. Lindley
"NUIT"
MANHATTAN COLLEGE 45 a.
"BEAUCHAMPS" M.E.Rutter 2 a.
"HAMPTON HOUSE"
CENTRAL AND
BROADWAY
Improvement Co.
FERRY
Dobbs Ferry Land
Loan Bros.
70 a.
PALMER AVE.
The Dobbs Ferry Land Improvement Co. Farm
D. O. Bradley 30 a.
"AGAWAM"
Gen. Samuel Thomas
Mrs. S.L.Tyers
Hiram Odell 21 a.
ARDSLEY PARK CO.
Jones
0   300

"I had a very happy childhood..."

Ann lee mac nicol's memories of Irvington, written in 1970, are personal and charming:

When I was three years old my family moved to Irvington, where we lived at the foot of West Clinton Avenue, right on the river front.

I had a very happy childhood. There were hills and trees, many places for us to play. Clinton Avenue in those days was a very popular place for coasting in the winter. To get our mail we would walk to the post office in the railroad station at Ardsley-on-Hudson. There was a board-walk from our place along the railroad to the Ardsley station.

Next to us, to the East, lived the William McAdoo family, former Secretary of the Treasury and son-in-law of President Woodrow Wilson. South, was the Phillip Schuyler estate, extending from Broadway to the River. Across Clinton Avenue were the wide meadows and lawns of the Luke place. Up Clinton Avenue was the "Octagonal House."

During the Summer afternoons we would walk down to the old Ardsley Club to see the Tally-Ho go by. A splendid sight, drawn by four or perhaps six horses prancing along driven by a top-hatted coachman. Two buglers, resplendant in red and white uniforms, tricorn hats with a feather waving in the breeze, sat high on the rear of the coach, blowing their long bugles from time to time . . . We were hoping some day that we would get a ride on the wonderful Tally-Ho, but we never did! However, we were always thrilled to watch it go by, a swirl of dust covering us as we waved gaily to the parasolled ladies and top-hatted gentlemen.

The old Ardsley Club was a very lively place. Summer evenings we children would lie in bed, and listen to the dance music as it wafted across the meadows . . .

The most splendiferous event of the whole Summer, for us children, was the Club's Fourth-of-July fireworks display. People came from all around. As soon as it became dusk we would go down to the railroad station, and join the crowd sitting on the railroad bank and piles of railroad ties waiting for the show to start. I have seen fireworks many times since, but to my childish mind, I have never seen any so beautiful.

The biggest event in the history of those days was the famous Hudson-Fulton Celebration in 1909. It lasted all Summer, and we along the river had reserved seats for the parade of probably all the finest yachts in America, beautifully decorated with lights and flags. The lighted yachts would glide up and down the river at night, and the nightboats, of which at that time there were

Every conceivable type of craft participated in the centennial of the famous voyage of Fulton's Clermont—canoes, yachts, Albany night boats and even a battleship

many, all lit up, would throw the gleam of their search lights along the banks of the river, when we would all jump up and wave as the light swept about us. It was the most lovely celebration in the history of the Hudson River.

In honor of the event, the Village of Irvington sponsored a great parade. Floats, bands,

A cooling sight as a float bearing the winter sled of the Broadway Line passed by

marching organizations, and fire departments marched along Broadway from Sunnyside Lane to the Irvington-Dobbs Ferry line. The Village Fathers arranged to hand out sandwiches and ice cream along the route. We children had a ball that day!

Somehow in those days the Summers seemed longer because so many things happened. There were such special treats as trips by excursion boat to Coney Island and Rockaway, sponsored by different village organizations. Whole families, pushing baby carriages loaded with babies and lunch baskets would walk up the Aqueduct, then down Main Street to the Village Dock to board the boat. Soon the boat would pull away, whistles tooting and flags flying, while we children tore from one side to the other to see Yonkers, New York City, the Statue of Liberty, wave at passing boats, and crowd the rail as she pulled into the Amusement Park. Our parents tried to

North River Line—Daylight New York to Albany. Low pressure steamboat

keep the picnic lunches until we went ashore, but I am afraid the salt air stimulated appetites, and the clamoring of children, "Mother, please, I'm hungry!" And father's gruff "Get away from those baskets!" As we well knew, when all the lunch was gone there were hot-dogs, taffy, spun sugar candy and many other tempting eatables at the Park. After a lively day in the Park the boat would return us to Irvington about ten o'clock in the evening. Then we would trudge up Main Street, the baby carriages filled with empty lunch baskets and sleeping babies while our parents lugged the youngest on their shoulders, and we older children dragged along in various stages behind.

I remember when I was quite small the Irvington Town Hall was built on Main Street. For many years the Town Hall was the center of Village activities, for dances, card parties, fairs and vaudeville shows, and a wonderful place to go for an evening's entertainment. The six boxes over the upper hall always intrigued me. I had visions of myself, in a feather boa leaning over the edge of the box, looking at the people below, while Caruso sang Pagliacci.

In later years I spent many a happy hour in the Guiteau Library [which was housed in

the Town Hall]. There were no movies or recreation centers, very few automobiles or airplanes. No doubt it was a different way of life compared with today, but we were happy and seemed to enjoy ourselves and keep busy.

ORDER OF DANCING
Part First

1.	WALTZ,	To our Trustees
2.	TWO-STEP,	To our Foreman
3.	WALTZ,	How's the baby carriage, Jimmy?
4.	TWO-STEP,	I'm Lonesome, Horace
5.	WALTZ,	The 3:10 is due, Henry
6.	TWO-STEP,	When is it coming off, Jack?
7.	WALTZ,	Concrete in the Hampshires, ask Jack
8.	TWO-STEP,	B'gosh its fierce
9.	WALTZ,	Shut off the water, Marty!
10.	TWO-STEP,	To our Exempts

INTERMISSION

From a Victorian graduation programme

School days

Irvington's first High School, built in the 1870's

Ellen Jane Mann is my name America is my nation Irvington is my dwelling Place Heaven is my Expectation the grass is green the ___ is red here lies my name when I am dead and gone forever EJM MAPS. ___ *Ellen Jane Mann March 2 1864*

Penned in Ellen J. Mann's geography book, 1864

Miss Margaret Tewey, with her pupils in 1875, was the first of a teaching family.

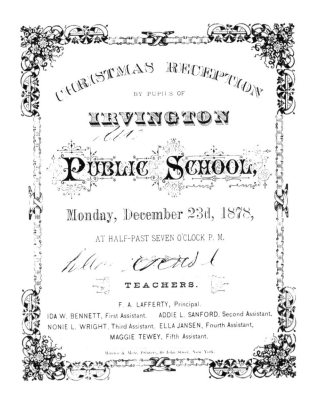

CHRISTMAS RECEPTION

BY PUPILS OF

IRVINGTON

Public School,

Monday, December 23d, 1878,

AT HALF-PAST SEVEN O'CLOCK P. M.

TEACHERS.

F. A. LAFFERTY, Principal.

IDA W. BENNETT, First Assistant.   ADDIE L. SANFORD, Second Assistant.

NONIE L. WRIGHT, Third Assistant,   ELLA JANSEN, Fourth Assistant,

MAGGIE TEWEY, Fifth Assistant.

Munroe & Metz, Printers, 60 John Street, New York.

READING SCRIPTURES.

OPENING HYMN.—Let Every Heart Rejoice, School.

RECITATION.—Santa Claus' Poor Spell,
Euphemia Leonard.

DIALOGUE.—Boys' Rights,   Four Boys.

RECITATION.—My Dolly,   Mamie Conney.

SONG.—Little Acts of Kindness,   Twenty-four Girls.

RECITATION.—A Girl's Idea of Columbus,
Eva Taylor.

DIALOGUE.—A Bevy of I's (Eyes),   Ten Girls.

CHORUS.—Greeting Song,   School.

RECITATION.—House-work,   Carrie Crisfield.

READING.—The Smack in School, Mamie McIntyre.

SONG.—The Danube River,   Four Girls.

RECITATION.—New Year's Greeting,   Richard Allan.

DIALOGUE.—Keep Posted,   W. Stoner and F. Egan.

RECITATION.—Girls' Rights,   Ella Gibbons.

SONG.—Snow Flakes,   Twenty Girls.

RECITATION.—Little Bennie,   Rose Kelly.

RECITATION.—Half-Way Doin's,   Dewey Menzies.

CHORUS.—Work, for the Night is Coming,   School.

RECITATION.—Edith Helps Things Along,
Mamie Greigg.

The pupils entertain, Christmas 1878

25TH ANNIVERSARY PROGRAMME

OPENING CHORUS—Ye Old Time Greeting Glee . . .

READING SCRIPTURE—Dr. Benjamin.

INVOCATION—Rev. J. A. Ingham.

WELCOME—President Board of Education
W. A. Burnham.

RECITATION AND SONG—Welcome. Primary Class.

RECITATION—Education. Mr. Edward Clark.

SONG—Three Jolly Sailor Boys . . .

RECITATION—They Ask Me Why I Am So Bad
Willie Owens.

ESSAY—History of the School. Miss Emma Knodel.

PIANO DUET—Miss Georgie Lord and Miss Janet
Hunter.

RECITATION—When the Teacher Gets Cross.
Harry Tewey.

CHORUS—Hither Fairies Trip . . .

RECITATION—Sparticus to the Gladiators
Mr. Irving M. Taylor, Jr.

SOLO—Life's Lesson. Mary Maitland.

RECITATION—Aunt Hetty's Idea of Matrimony
Miss Theresa Morgan.

READING—Selected. Mr. R. G. Abercrombie.

It is an ox. It is my ox.
Go up to it. I am to go.
So go ye up to it by me.

Lo! it is my ax. Is it so?
If it be my ax, I am to go to it.
Ah, it is my ax, so I go to it.

From "The Road to Learning" 1850

Teacher Margaret Tewey gets a raise to 700 dollars a year

This is to Certify, *That we have this day engaged Margaret M. Tewey (a duly licensed teacher) to teach in the Public Schools of District No. 2, town of Greenburgh, County of Westchester, for the term of twelve months, commencing September 1st 1892, at a compensation of Seven hundred dollars payable monthly. Within ten months.*

Irvington, N. Y.,

May 31 18,

W. S. Brunhan
Jno Dennis
James Mulligan

} TRUSTEES.

Third grade, East Irvington School, 1895

A school portrait in a gaslit classroom—1907. Seated rows, front to back: Near row: *Margaret Denton, Elizabeth Henry, Bertha Berger, Bertha McNeilly, Jennie Smith.* Second row: *Helen Dongan, Helen Stuart, Molly Hagen, Ella Hanyen, Maud Hazel Patterson, Unknown.* Third row: *Unknown, Mary O'Leary, Lulu Buckhout, Laura Dongan, Mary Lonergan, Theresa O'Leary.* Fourth row: *Unknown, William Sniffen, John Healy, Ruth Hanyen, Margaret Purcell, Emil Fassell.* Fifth row: *— O'Keefe, Edward Reynolds, Walter Elder, Arthur Elder, Leo Taaffe.* Standing around room, left to right: *Hubert Murray(?), Harry Tewey, Edmond Murphy, Kenneth Stuart, Raymond Gilligan, Dr. Gibbs (Principal), Mr. Bird (teacher), Agnes Murphy, Martha Raisch, Jennie Anderson, Miss Margaret Tewey (teacher), Anna Leonard, Nellie Kiernan, Isabel Duff, Margaret Lonergan, Lillian Wackwitz, Marion Roy, Miss Taft (teacher), Margaret McWilliam. The following were included on the rolls of these classes: Sarah Elliott, Elizabeth Knodel, Thomas McWilliam, Anna Robb, Cora Turrentine*

The kindergarteners at work, 1914

A group of 1913's High School students

(Opposite) The village in 1928

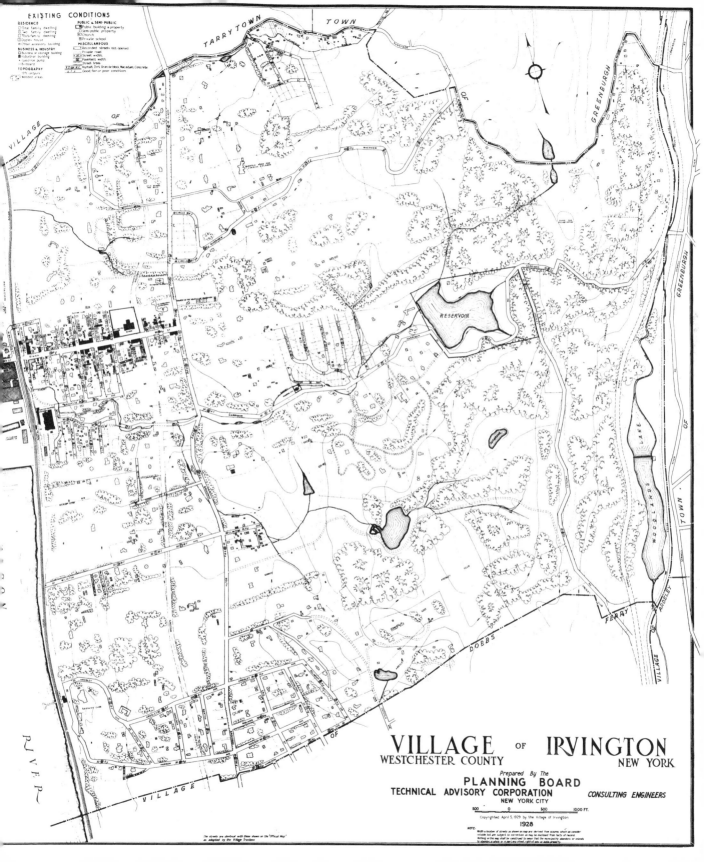

VILLAGE OF IRVINGTON

WESTCHESTER COUNTY   NEW YORK

Prepared By The

PLANNING BOARD
TECHNICAL ADVISORY CORPORATION
NEW YORK CITY

CONSULTING ENGINEERS

Copyrighted April 5, 1929 by the Village of Irvington

1928

In memory of those...

ON NO DAY OF THE YEAR does Irvington come together more meaningfully as a village than on Memorial Day. Carl Carmer describes it:

One way to see Irvington at its best is to walk over to Memorial Park on the morning of a national holiday—on Memorial Day, for instance. The music of the high school band will be throbbing over on Main Street, and soon the sound will be louder and nearer. The parade will turn into Dows Lane, and the Police and Fire Departments in their blue uniforms will be

Arthur C. Lord salutes on Memorial Day as a Scoutmaster of the Irvington Troop of the Boy Scouts of America

"We won!" Girl Scout Oak Troop #1 (1927) led by Miss Benjamin, photographed with ribbons won as County's best in "marching and appearance."

146

Fife and Drum leading the Village fathers in a Memorial Day parade in the early 1930's

marching in the lead. After them will be the war veterans, carrying the flag proudly. Then the ministers of the three churches, the Girl Scouts, the Boy Scouts and, at last, blasting away in march time, the band in green and white uniforms turns in front of the marching column. Mothers and fathers stand on the grass, enjoying the sight of their progeny marching by. Here, commuters to New York offices, whose week-day glimpses of Irvington are usually caught in the early morning or at dinner time, find happy companionship with their neighbors who work in the village. The whole view is so like a scene on the cover of a weekly American magazine that everyone feels a bit self-conscious, but at the same time more than a little proud.

A first lady of Irvington, Isabel K. Benjamin

147

*Official street map, Irvington, 1971. Opposite,
US Navy air view taken in February 1965 shows
an icy river*

148

Acknowledgements

Throughout the preparation of this book, the editors have drawn heavily on the knowledge, experience and encouragement of many individuals. They here list some of the persons, with the societies and other institutions they represent, and express their deep gratitude for the patient aid offered.

Edgar Bolduc, Jr., Vernelia Crawford, Anne MacNicol, Charles M. Pateman, 3rd, Clara Pearce, George Rowe, Jr., Elizabeth E. Smith, Walter W. Vail, William Van Leer.

Mimi Bronnes Bonney, W. Barton Eddison, Henri Fluchere, Dorothy Hagberg, Gordon Hendricks, J. Leonard leViness, Joseph Moore, Margaret C. Robertson, Mr. and Mrs. W. Wallace Ryan, Lynn Stevenson, Mrs. Stuart R. Stevenson, Mary M. Tewey, Adele M. Warnock, Alfred Woebcke

Patricia E. Smith and Elinor R. Bradshaw of Sleepy Hollow Restorations, Mrs. J. Floyd Smith and Harry E. Storm of the Historical Society of the Tarrytowns, Jane Devlin of Lyndhurst, of the National Trust for Historic Preservation, Anthony Corkill of the Hudson River Valley Commission, Howard Cross of Lord and Burnham, Nataly C. Baum of Downtown Gallery, Nancy Levy of Irvington Public Library and the Mayor and Trustees of the Village of Irvington.

Special Photographs by Mark Carolan, Carl Ramirez and Dan Berry. Drawings by Lauri Denyer.

Picture credits

List
of Maps

A rubbing of the gravestone of Susanah Ecker in Sleepy Hollow Cemetery. One of Irvington's early settlers, she lived and died in Wolfert's Roost

Index